I
like you

PROGRAM TRADING

PROGRAM TRADING

THE NEW AGE OF INVESTING

JEFFREY D. MILLER
WITH
MARA MILLER AND
PETER J. BRENNAN

J.K. LASSER INSTITUTE

New York

J.K. Lasser Institute

J.K. Lasser Institute
Simon & Schuster, Inc.
Gulf + Western Building
One Gulf + Western Plaza
New York, N.Y. 10023

J.K. Lasser, the J.K. Lasser Institute, and colophon are trademarks of Simon &
Schuster, Inc.

Distributed by Prentice Hall Trade Sales

1   2   3   4   5   6   7   8   9   10

Manufactured in the United States of America

Library of Congress Cataloging-in-Publication Data

Miller, Jeffrey.
   Program trading.

   Includes index.
   1. Program trading (Securities) I. Miller, Mara.
II. Brennan, Peter (Peter J.) III. J.K. Lasser
Institute. IV. Title.
HG4515.5.M55   1989   332.63'028'5   89-8141
ISBN 0-13-730318-1

We believe the research and interpretation by the authors and the J.K. Lasser Institute to be authoritative and will be of general help to readers. Readers are cautioned,
however, that this book is sold with the understanding that, although every care has
been taken in the preparation of the text, the Publisher is not engaged in rendering
legal, accounting, financial, or other professional service. Readers with specific problems are urged to seek the professional advice of a certified financial planner, an
accountant, or a lawyer.

Acknowledgments

pg. 2 Table One, Common Stocks: Total Returns, © Ibbotson, Roger G., and Rex A. Sinquefield, *Stocks, Bonds, Bills and Inflation* (SBBI), 1982, updated in *Stocks, Bonds, Bills and Inflation 1989 Yearbook*, Ibbotson Associates, Inc., Chicago. All rights reserved.

pg. 71 Excerpt from article entitled "Stocks, Funds, Cash Reserves Become an Important Ingredient in Performance" by Randell Smith, *The Wall Street Journal*, December 18, 1987, reprinted by permission of *The Wall Street Journal*, © Dow Jones & Company, Inc. (1987). All rights reserved worldwide.

pg. 72 Excerpt from article entitled "Recent Market Rally Saw Failure of Proven Stock-Picking Methods" by Barbara Donnelly, *The Wall Street Journal*, September 15, 1987, reprinted by permission of *The Wall Street Journal*, © Dow Jones & Company, Inc. (1987). All rights reserved worldwide.

pg. 77 Excerpt from *A Random Walk Down Wall Street*, 2nd Ed., by Burton G. Malkiel, copyright 1981, reprinted by permission of the publisher, W.W. Norton & Company, Inc., New York, New York.

pg. 98 Excerpt from article entitled "Packaged Goods" by Lenny Glynn and Saul Hansell, *Institutional Investor*, September 9, 1988, reprinted by permission of *Institutional Investor* (1988). All rights reserved worldwide.

pg. 106 Table of the 20 stocks that make up the Major Market index, entitled "A Real-Life Strategy For Making 14% Risk Free," *Business Week*, April 7, 1986, reprinted by permission of *Business Week*, © McGraw-Hill Inc. (1986). All rights reserved worldwide.

pg. 142 Table Nine, "Basic Series: Summary Statistics of Annual Returns 1926-1987," © Ibbotson, Roger G., and Rex A. Sinquefield, *Stocks, Bonds, Bills and Inflation* (SBBI), 1982, updated in *Stocks, Bonds, Bills and Inflation 1988 Yearbook*, Ibbotson Associates, Inc., Chicago. All rights reserved.

pg. 167 Figure Eight, "Wang Money Flow Stock Summary," furnished courtesy of Shark Service, Wang Financial Information Services Corp., New York, New York.

pg. 175 Figure Nine, page excerpt from *Current Consensus*, Zacks Estimate Service, December 30, 1988, reprinted by permission of Zacks Investment Research, Inc., Chicago, Illinois.

For Robert

CONTENTS ——————————————

——————————————

Contents

INTRODUCTION ───────────

The crash of October 1987 caught most investors completely by surprise. In its aftermath, there was a public perception that program trading and the new market instruments were to blame. Program trading still looms large in the public's consciousness of the events precipitating the crash. The pressures on the regulators and the markets have brought proposals for many restrictions on program trading, a few of which have been put in place (such as restricted use of the Designated Order Turnaround, or DOT, system under certain circumstances). Some brokerage firms have announced that they will no longer engage in index arbitrage (which, of course, uses program trading) for their own accounts, although they will continue to do so for their clients.

One company, the Advest Group of Hartford, Connecticut, a multioffice brokerage firm, took out a full-page advertisement in *The Wall Street Journal* on January 28, 1988. Headlined "Stop Program Trading," the ad urged readers to write to the heads of the SEC, of the NYSE and of the appropriate committees of the House and Senate. It also urged readers to ask their present brokers if they engaged in this practice and, if so, to exercise the "pocketbook vote" and move their business elsewhere, presumably to Advest.

None of the many studies produced before, during, or after the market crash have called for an outright ban on program trading. There appears to be a recognition that it is impossible to put the genie back in the bottle, even if that were desirable. In London, a study of the International Stock Exchange's performance during the crash concluded that the participants in the British stock market should increase their use of arbitrage and hedging techniques to prevent a repeat of the October crash. The British report found that an absence of arbitrage activity allowed a large discount to the cash index to develop, driving down the market. In Dublin, the Irish Futures and Options Exchange (IFOX) opened for business in 1988, undeterred by the crash, showing that even small capital markets appreciate the value of these instruments. In Japan, if the trading in futures on bonds in the largest futures market in the world is any indication, the 1988 introduction of stock futures will have enormous consequences for their market.

Program trading is but another tool in the investors' kit. It is the child of the modern age of high-speed communications and computerized stock trading, and it will not go away. Like any mechanism, it can be abused as well as used, and its potential for abuse must be addressed. We hope, in this book, to encourage further understanding of program trading and all the other modern forces (instruments, strategies, new actors, *et al.*) that have contributed to a transformation of the stock market. And we hope to show today's individual investor that, by understanding these forces, one can be in the right position at the right time to profit from the market's moves.

Chapter One ──────────────

VOLATILITY AND THE CRASH

There is no such thing as liquidity of investment for the community as a whole.
John Maynard Keynes

Before the 'Crash of '87'

When RMS *Titanic* foundered on a cold April night in 1912, survivors heard the doomed band on the sloping deck play a hymn. According to one of the ship's radio operators, it was not "Nearer My God to Thee," but rather "Autumn."

Investors might well take that theme as their own, for it is not April but October that is the cruelest month. "There is something in October that sets the

1

gypsy blood astir," a poet wrote, and might have added, "and sets the bears to roaring."

October of 1929 marked the beginning of the Great Depression, heralded by a 24 percent decline in the Dow Jones Industrial Average over two days, October 28 and 29. In October 1987 began—what? We don't yet know.

Table One

COMMON STOCKS: TOTAL RETURNS

1926	11.6%	1984	6.3%
1927	37.5%	1985	32.1%
1928	43.6%	1986	18.5%
1929	(8.4%)	1987	5.2%
1930	(24.9%)	1988	16.8%
1931	(43.3%)	1989	?
1932	(8.2%)	1990	?

SOURCE: SBBI (Stocks, Bonds, Bills and Inflation) 1988 Yearbook (Chicago: Ibbotson Associates, 1988) p. 150.

Such literary-historical thoughts may have crossed the collective mind of the financial markets early on the morning of Monday, October 19, 1987. People had been drawing parallels, however flawed, between summer 1929 and summer 1987. As Table One shows, the years leading up to 1929 had been good ones, with substantial returns on common stock investment. The same could be said for the years leading up to 1987.

But as the traders in the stock, futures and options markets around the country prepared for their day on October 19, 1987, more immediate and pressing concerns occupied their minds.

A Week of Apprehension

In retrospect, the previous week had been a tumultuous period, one of the most dramatic in the modern history of the financial markets. The markets closed on Friday, October 15, in a "waterfall," as one broker put it, 108 points down. That followed a week of record double-digit declines that stripped some 300 points from the average. From its high of 2,722 on August 25, the market had slid with increasing acceleration nearly 500 points, almost 20 percent off its peak.

More ominously, markets abroad in London, Tokyo, and Hong Kong, whose boom had paralleled that of the U.S. markets, had declined before the New York markets even opened on October 19. Overseas markets had observed the decline in New York the week before and especially the slide on Friday, which occurred after the overseas markets had closed. As New York opened on Monday, it was already late Monday evening in the Far East, and London's Monday trading was five hours along. Tokyo, which had closed down 2.3 percent on Monday, Tokyo time, would not reopen for hours. Hong Kong, having closed down 11.3 percent on this same day, the 19th, would later decide to remain closed and would not reopen that week. The shutdown did not relieve the pressure, though it did allow time to arrange a bailout of the futures market. When Hong Kong reopened, the Hang Seng Index (Hong Kong's version of the Dow Jones) fell 25 percent in the first thirty minutes of trading. The closing of the exchange did not help stem the stock market decline, and Hong Kong ended as far down as U.S. markets.

New York, as usual, was the world pacesetter. As New York's markets plunged from Friday the 16th onwards, markets around the world followed, the wave of collapse following the sun westward and backwashing to still-open markets in Europe. (London would finish Monday down 10.1%, the latter part of that day's drop in response to New York's falling market.) For the first time, events graphically demonstrated to both the professional and individual investor that the notion of a Global Market was a reality.

U.S. stocks that trade around the world on foreign exchanges were already feeling the selling pressure that was building in the U.S. One fund, the Fidelity Group, was trying to "get ahead of the expected selling on the NYSE by selling in London." Fidelity sold just under $90 million of stocks in London and was trying to meet its commitments to shareholders who had redeemed shares on the previous Friday at what the shareholders had expected would be Friday's closing price.

Worse, hanging over the market's opening was an enormous quantity of sell orders representing billions of dollars that had accumulated over the weekend of October 17–18. This awaited New York and Chicago traders as they braced for Monday's opening bell. The bulk of this overhang only became apparent toward the end of the preceding week; and, being difficult to precisely measure, it was all the more frightening.

Clearly, Monday, October 19, 1987, was to be no ordinary trading day. On that day, the Dow Jones Industrial Average suffered its worst one-day loss ever, plunging by 508 points. The percentage drop, 22.6 percent, was nearly twice that of the worst day prior to this date—Black Monday, October 28, 1929.

On October 19, 1987, trading volume on the New York Stock Exchange topped an incredible 600 million shares—1.5 million shares per minute of trading throughout the day. Unlike earlier wild swings of the Dow Jones Index, in which the percentage variation was negligible, the Dow's decline was disastrous by any standard. A 100-point-plus bounce the next day (the market's greatest single-day gain ever) on ever greater volume momentarily diverted attention from a financial system seemingly on the edge of chaos and total collapse.

Analysts, investors, and just about everyone else went looking for explanations—something that might account for the dramatic fall. More than a few went hunting up villains. One likely suspect was program trading, a technique that had come to symbolize all that was new in the securities markets.

Program trading encompasses a variety of techniques, but, simply stated, it may be defined as buying and selling groups of stocks rather than individual stocks. What is significant to note for our introductory purpose is the impact program trading can have on the total market movement because of the shares that make up the particular program. Program trading had been taking the heat for market volatility for several years. In the aftermath of October 19, when explanations were sought for the sudden point drop in the Dow, program trading became a convenient target.

A correction in the heretofore soaring bull market of 1987 had been long expected. Many observers felt that equities (on the average) had risen to such a point that they were out of sync with any reasonable criterion of value. As Figure One shows, price earnings ratios had risen dramatically from the early 1980s. In the long bull market that began in 1982, the Dow Jones Index had climbed past 1000, then past 2000 for the first time ever. Volume of trading had kept pace, growing to a level of 200 million shares a day.

During its rise, the market fluctuated, as it always has and always will. While one-day 100-point moves had not yet occurred, twenty- and thirty-point shifts were not unusual. People continued to track the absolute level of the Dow Jones, but it took a while for them

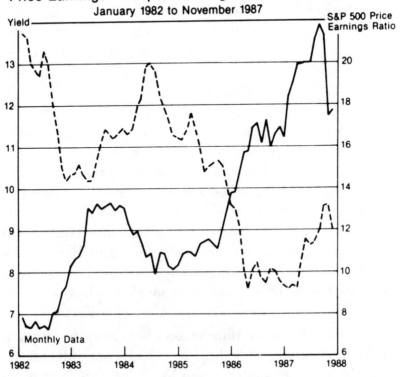

U.S. MARKET
Price Earnings Multiple vs Long Term Bond Yield
January 1982 to November 1987

SOURCE: "Report of The Presidential Task Force on Market Mechanisms," January, 1988.

Figure One

to realize that a twenty-point move when the index is at 2000 is not as significant as the same move when the index is at 800. The crash of 1929, after all, involved a two-day decline totalling only 69 points in the Dow Jones Index.

The market of 1987 was different from that of 1929 in many respects. Unlike 1929, no frenzy of speculation by individual investors operating on thin margins drove this market. The 1987 market, instead, featured large pools of assets concentrated in the hands of retirement fund sponsors. For example, on September 30, 1987, General Motors had pension assets of $40 billion. The top 100 retirement plans in the U.S. had $1 trillion in assets. Then, there were a host of players—risk arbitrageurs, corporate buyers of other companies, operators of leveraged-buy-out funds—that comprised the primary agents in the merger-and-acquisition hyperactivity of the 1980s. Finally, new stock market strategies which used program trading techniques, such as portfolio insurance and index arbitrage, had been developed. These factors all combined to create new patterns of stock market behavior.

Perhaps the least understood phenomenon was portfolio insurance, a technique whose possible effects were not contemplated, even by many who were using it in the summer of 1987, when the Dow soared. Portfolio insurance is used by fund managers as a way of hedging (controlling) risks in markets. Of the assets allocated in any fund, stocks represent the opportunity for the highest return (compared to bonds and T-bills) but with the most risk attached. Any manager naturally would be attracted to a way of staying in stocks while limiting the fund's exposure to wide swings in the stock market. Portfolio insurance is a mathematically based technique that directs managers to buy stocks (or sell their equivalents) in the futures market if they begin to increase in price and to sell them if they begin to fall.

Both are hedges against the market's unpredictability. The manager knows that if the market should rise, at least he or she will get some percentage of the gain; and if it should drop, one will have reduced the loss before it becomes too great. At times, this strategy may involve frequent entering and exiting the market—a whipsawing that can become very expensive. It's a price one is willing to pay, however, in exchange for the confidence to keep the higher percentage of the portfolio in stocks.

In the fall of 1987, approximately $90 billion of pension assets had been covered by portfolio insurance in the U.S. stock and futures markets. During the summer, fund managers had continued to buy or hold stocks, believing themselves to be successfully hedged. These buys—or a dearth of sales—contributed to sending the Dow up to its dizzying heights. What was not taken into consideration at the time, however, was that the corresponding instructions-to-sell orders—on the stock futures—were already in place, in the form of portfolio insurance, in quantities of tens of billions of dollars' worth of stock. If and when the stock market declined sharply, the snowballing effect would be enormous.

But this was not foreseen by most stock market participants and observers. As the summer of 1987 turned into early fall, the Dow topped 2700, and near-euphoria was the order of the day in the American marketplace.

What had already begun to trouble some people was market volatility, both its increasing frequency, and, it sometimes seemed, its sheer unpredictability. On certain days during the year, specifically those on which two index options expired—on the American Stock Exchange and the Chicago Board of Options Exchange, plus index futures on the Chicago Mercantile Exchange—the market went into paroxysms.

Index futures and options had burst onto the scene in 1982–83. Options on stocks (the right to buy or sell stocks) had been trading for a long time, while futures (making a commitment now to buy or sell at some future time) had existed on commodities but never on stocks. Now came along two new derivatives: stock futures and options on an entire basket, or index, of stocks. What was also new was their method of settlement on expiration days. Instead of actually taking delivery (or making delivery, in the case of a seller) of the stock shares, stock futures and index options were settled on a cash basis, as though ownership of the shares had changed hands, without that formal exchange ever actually happening. Expiration dates occurred at varying times, but always on a Friday. On four Fridays of the year, the expirations of both the major index options and the major index futures coincide. Those days, the third Friday of the last month in each quarter, became known as Triple Witching Hour days, because enormous buying and selling of the shares of stocks that comprised the indexes occurred within the final hour—indeed, constituted the final trade of that day.

Witching-hour volatility began early in the 1982-to-present bull market, as some firms learned how to play the futures markets in Chicago against the securities markets in New York through the medium of index arbitrage.

Arbitrage is the practice of taking advantage of price disparities for the same item or object in two different markets. If a particular stock, for example, sells in London for $100.00 and in Chicago for $101.00, the arbitrageur profits from selling the stock in Chicago while buying it in London.

Index arbitrage is like classic arbitrage except that instead of taking advantage of disparities between the prices of the same stock but in two different markets, the index arbitrageur plays off the difference in prices of the index derivatives (futures or options) and the basket of stocks underlying the index. If, for instance, the Standard & Poor's 500 Index (like the Dow, a representative group of stocks) future were selling considerably above the value of the actual stock 500 Index, the arbitrageur would sell the future while simultaneously buying the actual shares in the index. "Considerably above" in this context means higher than the fair value of the future, which is calculated on a cash-and-carry basis. (Cash-and-carry analysis compares stock dividend yields with Treasury bill yields.) If, on the other hand, the index future were trading *below* its fair value, the arbitrageur would buy the future and sell the basket of stocks. In both instances, a profit is locked in once the buy and sell have been executed. On Triple Witching Hour days, traders whose futures contracts were closed out by the event of expiration rushed to either buy back or sell out huge quantities that they

11

had previously bought our sold against the futures. As the flood of orders for these market-on-close trades hit the exchanges at the end of the day, at one time, each expiration day brought intense public attention to index arbitrage and program trading.

As more and more traders began to do index arbitrage, from 1982 onward, the markets became accustomed to the results of that activity and its accompanying technique, program trading. More troubling, though, was the occasional and unexpected appearance of sudden, great, and unexplained volatility on *non*-Triple Witching Hour days. Because investors had witnessed the impact of program trading and, specifically, of index arbitrage, on Triple Witching Hour days, many now held those activities and techniques responsible for the non-Triple Witching day swings.

The Curtain Raiser

The first events to garner people's attention occurred on September 11 and 12, 1986. Though several instances of days with wide swings in the indexes had occurred over the preceding months, in addition to those swings seen on Triple Witching days, September 11 and 12 were the first warning tremors signalling a geological shift in the marketplace that would culminate in the cataclysm of October 19, 1987.

September 11, 1986, a Thursday, looked to be like any other trading day. The previous sessions had seen the indexes declining, but nothing alarming had happened. The Dow Jones had fallen from a high of 1920 the previous week, to close at just over 1880 on Wednesday. As they prepared for market opening on Thursday, the 11th, investors had little reason to expect anything but more of the same, or maybe even a turnaround. To most observers, the market seemed merely to be digesting the gains of previous weeks and was now marking time, preparing to resume its upward march.

The opening, however, indicated that this would be no ordinary day. The averages jumped off the cliff immediately and never looked back all day. Within half an hour, the Dow dropped twenty points, levelled off for an hour or so, then resumed its decline with a vengeance, down almost seventy points by 11:30 A.M. A brief rally carried it up through the noon hour, but after lunchtime, it was down again, ending the day 86 points off.

Even as investors counted up their losses and wondered what had hit them, they told themselves that though the point loss was unprecedented, the percentage change was not: a 4.6% drop was rare, but it had happened before. Perhaps it was a figure that could be tolerated.

On Friday, the market opened steady and moved slightly upward. By 11 A.M., however, traders panicked, and the average plunged fifty points. Then it rallied, regaining nearly all the day's losses, only to dribble off in the final hours to a net loss on the day of

34 points. Total loss for the two days was now 120 points, the biggest two-day damage ever to date, on what was then huge volume: 240 million shares on Thursday and 237 million shares on Friday.

Although both investors and regulators were accustomed to seeing such volatility on Triple Witching Fridays, they had not expected to find it on ordinary trading days. To be sure, as J. P. Morgan once observed, "The market will fluctuate." But this much? "What is happening to the financial markets?" "Are the markets now out of control and wholly unpredictable?" These were some of the questions being asked, in bewilderment, after September 11 and 12.

One school of economic thought accused index arbitrage of creating wide swings in the indexes, while another school defended the practice, crediting index arbitrage with having created liquidity, not volatility. A follow-up report by the Securities and Exchange Commission tended to support the latter view, asserting that index arbitrage *magnified but did not cause* [our emphasis] the precipitous drop in the stock market.

The SEC report did not appear until March 1987, and by then a second tremor—another tumultuous session on Friday, January 23, an otherwise ordinary trading day—again had shaken the financial community. The SEC report noted the events of January 23 (which, though a Friday, was not a Witching Hour day) in an addendum and promised that a full report would follow. If ever that subsequent study was begun,

14

it was no doubt set aside, if not jettisoned altogether, by the events of October 19.

The Compression of Time

The SEC report, based on dozens of interviews with traders in the equity and commodity markets, plus a painstaking study of every trade made on those two days, concluded that the reason for the precipitous decline on September 11 and 12 was not index arbitrage or portfolio insurance and its techniques of program trading, but market and economic fundamentals.

The SEC study found that the market at the time had "topped out," that investors were uneasy over several fundamental market factors and that the market was about to turn downward as a result of those factors. The SEC based that conclusion on its observation that it took the indexes several weeks to return to their pre-sell-off levels.

On expiration days, the indexes may show great volatility, ending the day either up or down, but they tend to return to previous levels on the next Monday. The Commission reasoned that the pattern that emerged throughout subsequent trading sessions after September 11 and 12 was not at all like the one that followed expiration days and that, therefore, the cause could not be technical in nature. A neat induction, but a fallacious one. It does not necessarily follow that because the fall did not bounce back afterwards, it had been nontechnical and therefore fundamental in origin. If the climb—the Dow Jones reaching its new high—*had* been technical in origin (for example, caused by the adoption by investors of a set of strategies that had nothing to do with fundamentals), then indeed the subsequent fall could be technical in nature.

The SEC, however, didn't see it that way, concluding that "the magnitude of the September decline was a result of changes in investors' perceptions of fundamental economic conditions, rather than artificial forces arising from index-related trading strategies."[1]

A corollary to its conclusion was the SEC's finding that the decline was compressed into a shorter, more severely felt period of time because of the development of modern communications systems and computer technology. In both its March 1987 report and again in its larger analysis in February 1988, *The October 1987 Market Break*, the Commission stated:

> While it did not appear that index-related trading artificially changed stock prices, the Division found that index strategies, particularly arbitrage, were instrumental in the rapid transmission of changed investor perceptions, usually reflected first in future prices, to individual stock prices. Accordingly, the Division found that index arbitrage may have condensed the time period in

[1] "The Role of Index-Related Trading in the Market Decline on September 11 and 12, 1986," A Report by the U.S. Securities and Exchange Commission, Division of Market Regulation, March 1987, Executive Summary.

which the September 11 and 12 market decline occurred.[2]

This finding implies that it was the speed with which the information (or "changed perceptions") was transmitted to the marketplace (and was then transformed into action, *i.e.*, selling) that caused such unsettling volatility.

It is generally acknowledged that modern communications and computer technology not only make the size and breadth of today's financial markets possible, but also make them more efficient and liquid by quickly placing more information in the hands of more people. By processing information rapidly, automation compresses time, allowing data to flow as fast as the processing system (itself automated) can handle it. Events that once worked themselves out in hours, days, or weeks now do so in minutes or hours.

Here we come to the heart of the issue: Is a market that has been made more efficient and liquid by advancing technology also more subject to unsettling volatility because advancing technology compresses time? Market commentators believe that to be true. We disagree. It is true that technology has made markets more efficient and liquid, and it is also true that technology compresses time. But as Figure Two illustrates, there is no evidence that today's markets are more vol-

---

[2] "The October 1987 Market Break," A Report by the Division of Market Regulation, U.S. Securities and Exchange Commission, February 1988, pp. 1–9.

60 DAY HISTORICAL VOLATILITY
S&P 500 Index

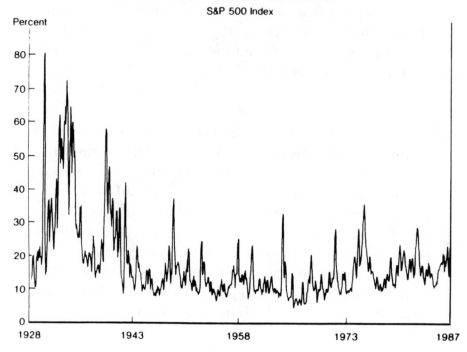

SOURCE: "Report of The Presidential Task Force on Market Mechanisms," January, 1988.

Figure Two

atile than they were in the past (much less that compressed time created this alleged volatility). The standard measurements of variation—comparing one period's price fluctuations with another period's price fluctuations—show no volatility increase.

Indeed, in the past, "slow" information made for more volatility. Consider the days of the Pony Express, when the fastest means of getting information from one side of the country to the other took weeks. News, good or bad, trickled out. Even when the news reached a distant point, dissemination to the community at large was slow, uncertain, and often inaccurate. By the time telegraph and train replaced the horse and rider, news still went first to the privileged few. In such an environment, fair, accurate and timely pricing of equities was impossible; those who had the information first had the advantage.

In the good old days, then, information came into the marketplace slowly. Those who received the information first knew that the news, whether good or bad, would have more of an unsettling effect on price as that news went out to more and more people. Action by buyers or sellers would be stretched out over a longer period of time, which is itself a destabilizing factor on price. In order to be able to withstand the impact of that delayed, spreading information, buyers or sellers would demand bigger "cushions." A prospective buyer of a stock, for instance, would want a larger discount, as protection against the effects on the price of that stock that slowly spreading bad news would have. One was likely to see larger percentage changes in stock prices in those good old days than one sees now.

So why do commentators and regulators continue to believe otherwise? We think the explanations for volatility lie elsewhere, as we explain in detail later in this chapter. But the fact remains that occasions of extreme volatility *have* occurred in the modern marketplace in the last few years, particularly those highly volatile days that occurred in September 1986 and October 1987. Investors are badly shaken as a result. January 23, 1987, wasn't the earthquake that October would be, but it was a large indicator, and a day worth noting. At one point during that day, the Dow Jones Index dropped 114 points in 70 minutes. At the closing bell the Dow was down over 44 points for the day, with a record volume of 302.4 million shares—on a non-expiration day.

January 23, 1987, was a harrowing day for traders in both Chicago and New York, as well as a nail-biting time for millions of individual investors standing on the sidelines, wondering what the professionals were doing to their life savings. As it happened, the wild swings had no lasting effect on the market, which continued its march to its August 25 high. But taken in concert with the previous volatility of September and the now-tamed Witching Hours days, this instability began to cause great uneasiness in the financial community. People like things to happen in an orderly manner, if not a predictable one. John Maynard Keynes said it well:

> Investment becomes reasonably "safe" for the individual investor over short periods . . . if he can fairly rely on there being no breakdown in the convention and on his therefore having an opportunity to revise his judgement and change his

investment, before there has been time for much
to happen.[3]

January 23, 1987, became history, literally no more
than a postscript in the SEC's report on September 11
and 12, 1986: "The trading on January 23 highlights
the possibility of dramatic intra-day price movements
similar to that which occurred on September 12, and
raises significant market structure questions."[4]

We have already seen how program trading came to
be identified with the volatility of Witching Hour expiration days. Ironically, that volatility abated when the
SEC required index arbitrageurs to disclose ahead of
time their planned stock purchases and sales for expiration dates. This confirms our point that more information leads to a more smoothly operating market. In
light of what we now know about events in October, it's
unfortunate that disclosure of information about other
kinds of strategies, portfolio insurance chief among
them, was not required.

Witching Hour volatility disappeared, but other
days' volatility did not. Some observers, such as John
Phelan, President of the New York Stock Exchange,
had an inkling of potential market instability and
raised the specter of a "market meltdown." According

---

[3] John Maynard Keynes, *The General Theory of Employment,
Interest, and Money* (New York: Harcourt, Brace, Jovanovich,
1964), p. 153.
[4] "The Role of Index-Related Trading in the Market Decline on
September 11 and 12, 1986," *op. cit.*, p. 28.

to this scenario, some negative news would send the market into a downturn. As index futures fell to a discount from fair value, accelerated stock selling would take place as arbitrageurs began to trade. The acceleration of stock selling would drive the futures even lower, which would produce, in turn, even more stock selling. Adding to this freefall would be sales from portfolio insurance programs. The market decline would be massive and overwhelming, far surpassing events of September 1986 and January 1987.

Fearful of this specter, the New York Stock Exchange engaged former U.S. Attorney General Nicholas deB. Katzenbach to examine the impact of program trading on the markets.[5] The conclusions of the study exonerated program trading as a cause of market instability. "The problems are not caused by programs," Katzenbach wrote. But though he exonerated program trading, he missed finding the right focus: the strategies that get played out through program trading. Portfolio insurance triggers the sale of futures, which leads to the sale of stocks in the form of a program trade. The active agent is not the program trade but rather the strategy of portfolio insurance. As we shall see, the breakdown of program trading on October 19 ironically added to the turbulence created by portfolio insurance as portfolio-insurance strategists became more desperate to sell.

---

[5] "An Overview of Program Trading and Its Impact on Current Market Practices," by Nicholas deB. Katzenbach, Esq. A Study Commissioned by the New York Stock Exchange, December 21, 1987.

Instead, Katzenbach first looked at "the impact of program trading" (which, after all, was what he had been asked to study). When that provided no answers, Katzenbach switched his lens to the structural differences between stocks and futures and their regulatory histories. As a result, his study missed an opportunity to alert investors to the threat posed by the strategies implemented through program trading.

The Earthquake

Everyone's worst fears materialized on October 19, when the market fell over 500 points. The next day, the New York Stock Exchange was within minutes of shutting down, and nearly all the futures exchanges did not function for at least part of the day on October 20.

Program trading was stopped, initially because stock specialists on the floor of the NYSE, overwhelmed by volume, were unable to handle orders received over the high-speed computerized order routing system called the Designated Order Turnaround system (DOT, now known as SuperDOT). Next, the Stock Exchange requested that program trading stop using the DOT system altogether. Because there was no program trading, many of the normal buyers of futures refused to enter the market. They'd only be willing to buy futures if they could do arbitrage by selling stocks through program trades. That route was effectively blocked. Portfolio-insurance strategists, relying on the futures market to control their risks, found little liquidity and bad pricing. The Presidential Task Force assigned to study the Crash said in its report (called "The Brady Report" after its Chairman, Nicholas F. Brady):

> Contributing greatly to this freefall was the lack of index arbitrage buying which would normally have been stimulated by the huge discount of futures to stock. At its opening (on October 20), the NYSE had prohibited broker-dealers from using the DOT system to execute index arbitrage orders for their own accounts. . . the primary linkage between the two markets had been disconnected.[6]

Though the official studies put the beginning of the debacle at Wednesday, October 14, there is strong evidence that the fuse had been lit earlier. An internal paper of Miller Tabak Hirsch + Co. dates the beginning to Monday, October 12, when one of the largest, most active firms, Salomon Brothers, announced the closing of its municipal bond department, the layoff of 800 employees, and a cut in earnings. At about this time, the yields on the 30-year Treasury bonds rose above 10 percent, foretelling higher returns on debt instruments and rendering low-yielding stocks less attractive. October 12 was a quasi-holiday (Columbus Day). The stock market was open, but the money markets were closed, and bonds did not trade. The bond

---

[6] "Report of The Presidential Task Force on Market Mechanisms," January 1988, p. 40.

futures market was open but very quiet. The stock market itself was quiet and down 10.77 points.

In retrospect it appears the markets were waiting for a trigger that would cause them to regroup. It came in the form of disappointing trade figures on the morning of October 14, followed by word that a Congressional committee had proposed a bill to eliminate tax benefits associated with the financing of corporate takeovers. Since much of the market rise had been fueled by take-over stocks, the Congressional initiative was a particularly negative development. Overnight, lenders who finance corporate acquisitions became loath to lend money in an unsettled legislative environment. Take-over stocks led the market down. The DJIA fell 95.46 points (then a record) on the 14th alone. In such a down market, portfolio insurance sell programs began to kick in.

On Friday, October 16, portfolio insurance programs mandated that several billion worth of stock or futures had to be sold. That day, the DJIA lost 108 points, another record. Over the three days, Wednesday through Friday, the average lost 250 points, more than 10 percent. People were more than nervous; they were on the edge of panic.

The Brady Report gives an example of the effect portfolio insurance had.

> One portfolio insurance client had followed exact-ly the instructions of the adviser during the Wednesday to Friday period. Over the weekend,

> the advisor informed the client that, based on Friday's market close, it should sell on Monday 70 percent of its remaining equities in order to conform to the parameters of its insurance model . . . The typical portfolio insurance model calls for stock sales in excess of 20 percent of a portfolio in response to a 10 percent decline in the market.[7]

Up to $90 billion of equity assets were under portfolio insurance administration at this time. Though close observers of the markets were aware that sizable portfolio insurance had built up, no one knew if (and when) it would kick in all at once. Because of the many forms and plans of portfolio insurance, with differing triggerpoints, floors, and time horizons, there was no one person or group of observers or actors in possession of all the relevant information.

The form of portfolio insurance we have been talking about is called dynamic hedging. Another way to insure a portfolio is to buy put options. If you own a put option, you own the right to sell the stocks at a prefixed price. In this case, the put options are purchased and the stocks retained. You never have to sell out your stocks. The portfolio manager (or you) recovers any decline in the value of the stocks from the increased value of the puts. In the dynamic hedging model, on the other hand, you must constantly adjust and rebalance your positions, reducing or increasing the amount of stock owned. At some point, the model

---

[7] "Report of The Presidential Task Force on Market Mechanisms," January 1988, p. 29.

may require that the entire portfolio be sold. This insurance strategy is computer-model driven and automatic.

With the market down ten percent in three days we estimate that the insurance programs required that funds sell a minimum of $12 billion and perhaps as much as $18 billion worth of stock by the close of business on Friday the 16th. In fact, they had sold only $4 billion. As the market continued to fall, the models required sales of between $20 billion and $30 billion in equities. This was an enormous bulge to come to market on Monday morning.

Almost all commentators on the crash have noted that only 15 percent of the dollar value of volume on both the New York Stock Exchange and the futures markets on those days was due to portfolio insurance. Yet, if we look at the percentage of public sell orders, say, in the futures markets on October 19, that proportion was closer to 50 percent.

In sum, these huge amounts of stock overhanging the market coupled with large sales by some mutual funds, which needed to raise cash to meet redemption demands by their shareholders, put unprecedented pressure on the markets over these five trading days.

The truly striking aspect of the entire debacle was how a few players in the market were responsible for most of the activity. One mutual fund sold over a billion dollars' worth of equities. One pension fund sold over a billion in 13 separate waves of selling, effectively

27

knocking the pins out from under the market every time it tried to get up.

The total volume for October 19 was 604 million shares; for October 20 it was 608 million. Despite these large numbers, the fact is that most investors neither bought nor sold, but rather sat on the sidelines. The entire crash had been played out by the large institutions.

The stock markets proved finite, illiquid, and inefficient. The world learned that institutions exist that are large enough to have the resources to overwhelm the markets and dry up liquidity. There is indeed no such thing as liquidity of investment for the community as a whole, when the entire community comes to the same side of the market simultaneously, and the marketplace has no prior information that this liquidity demand could, even in theoretical terms, be placed on it.

Besides mutual funds and portfolio insurers, another agent was at work: aggressive trading institutions. (We believe many of these were Wall Street firms working with their own capital.) On one day alone, they accounted for 9 percent of volume. On October 16, these traders sold $1.4 billion worth of stock, and bought $1.1 billion. Official accounts have had little to say about these trading institutions but we believe they merit more attention than has so far been received.

These are traders with no long investment-time horizon but with enormous amounts of capital committed to no purpose but to earn short-term profits, like a scalper in the S&P 500 trading pits. They allocate capital not on value, but only to where it can go for the quickest profit. Where other players in the market, such as the pension funds, portfolio insurers, and mutual funds, trade for value and to protect and enhance assets for long-term purposes, the aggressive trading houses have no interest but to scalp profits. They do add liquidity to the marketplace as, in the case of Wall Street firms, they use that capital to facilitate trades on behalf of their customers. If there is fault, it lies in the failure of the markets to recognize the potential weight of this pool of capital and the manner in which it most probably will be employed.

In the crash, that capital had no desire to sacrifice itself. Even stock exchange specialists, who are charged with the responsibility for supporting markets, had no desire to do that. These aggressive trading institutions, which have such close proximity to the market, could begin to see the shadow of portfolio insurance and thus were quick to take advantage of it. Perhaps it is the reflexive nature of predators to do just that when faced with ample prey.

Chapter Two

TODAY'S STYLE OF INVESTMENT AND HOW WE GOT THERE

Predictions and the Stock Market

Prediction is not a science, never has been. Trying to find surefire ways of knowing and saying what will happen is an age-old phenomenon, older than the Roman Empire. This brings us to the central question about any forecasting system: Is it based on a rationale sufficient to gain our confidence? Historically, there may have been a strong correlation, for example, between the length of women's skirts and the direction of the stock market, but that random connection is hardly a good enough reason to buy and sell stocks. Calpurnia's warning to her husband Julius Caesar not to go to the Roman Senate on that fateful day, based on a dream she had had the night before, was no more remarkable for its specificity and felt certainty than it was for the alacrity with which it was ignored.

Today's popular stock market predictors may make many claims foretelling events and may chime in with "I-told-you-so's" after the fact. Appearing to have been right, after the fact, is also an age-old phenomenon; even the ancient Greeks knew how to hedge their predictions through words that, later, might be able to be construed so as to prove them correct. But as serious analysts and investors, we will ignore them even if, like Caesar, ignoring their advice leads to our demise. For Caesar was right (even though he lost his life that day) to refuse to base his actions on a dream.

One of the most difficult truisms for an investor to accept—and yet it must be accepted because it is true—is that a good strategy may produce a less than desired outcome. Contained within a good strategy may always be a small probability for a bad turn of events. We keep that small probability in mind, but we act based upon the concept of expected outcome.

The forces that demonstrably move the market today are many, complex, and non-predictable. Yet like those who have preceded us, we continue to seek near-scientific ways by which we can reasonably gauge outcomes. One of the first developed models by which stock market behavior could be viewed, if not entirely predicted, is the Dow Jones Industrial Index. Commonly referred to as "the Dow," this index is a list of the stocks of thirty large, blue-chip U.S. companies. It

1894

was devised in ~~1984~~ by Charles H. Dow, editor of *The Wall Street Journal*, as a tool for measuring the performance of the entire stock market based on the price movements of (then) only eleven stocks. In 1928, the number of stocks in the index was increased to thirty. Those thirty were seen as a valid "sample," in much the same way that a sample of, say, 1500 voters is a statistically useful indicator of how our entire nation will vote.

From the development of this index grew the Dow Theory, based on Dow's assertion that the market has three separate movements all happening at the same time (a narrow day-to-day movement, a long swing of two weeks to a month, and a major trend of about four years' time) and that within major uptrends of the market averages, intermediate downtrends will occur that closely resemble a large portion of the uptrend, then recover and go on to exceed the previous high. Should the recovery stop short of the previous high, the market is deemed to be heading for a major downward slide.

The Dow Theory remains the basis for much of today's technical analysis of the stock markets. The reason we pay attention to it is precisely that: If many investors base their actions on a known formula, that model of prediction easily can become self-fulfilling in the short run. This phenomenon often occurs today: "hot" stock market forecasters become overnight media stars with large followings; the actions of the followers then are quite noticeable in the market and would seem to prove the forecaster correct. . . . for a while.

In today's market, different philosophies mark the different approaches to choosing stocks. *Technical analysts*, or *technicians*, believe that everything that can be known—or needs to be known—about a security is reflected in its price. They then interpolate current price movement in relation to previous price movements so as to plot the trend of future price movement. Some technical analysts study not only the price movement but also volume or even such esoterica as velocity of price change. Certain technical analysts are called *chartists*, and they use line, bar, and point-and-figure charts to search for patterns they believe will predict trends and movements.

Fundamentals analysts, or *fundamentalists*, on the other hand, study the basic facts about a company in order to estimate its future health and prosperity. They develop earnings forecasts and estimate changes, if any, that may occur in the price-earnings ratio of particular companies. Changes in price-earnings ratios can usually be associated with developments occurring either in the broad market (for example, rising interest rates generally lead to lower ratios and vice versa) or changes in the individual stock (for example, an increasing rate of earnings growth generally leads to higher ratios) or both. By combining a forecast of earnings with predicted changes in price-earnings ratios, the analyst calculates a future price, which is then compared to current price, in order to compute the expected return from an investment.

In the early 1950s, academicians and scholars began to use statistical methods to create theories about the behavior of the stock market. They applied probability theory to the behavior of securities markets as a whole and mathematically related the rate of return of a stock, a portfolio, or the entire market to the degree of risk in each. This approach revealed the expected level of return at a certain level of risk for any stock or portfolio, or, conversely, the level of risk that must be assumed for a certain level of return.

For some time, *Modern Portfolio Theory* (MPT) remained simply theory, untested in the real world. No one actually constructed portfolios based on MPT because, first, the tools for doing so either did not exist or were too expensive for most managers; and, second, there was enormous resistance to this type of stocks-in-the-aggregate thinking by fund managers. In the ensuing decades, though, computers of greater capacity have become widespread, making easy the acquisition, measurement, and manipulation of data that is required for putting Modern Portfolio Theory into practice. Most portfolio managers today, whether consciously or not, work within the framework of MPT. Even those who don't use it themselves to obtain their results find their performance results judged by MPT standards. Modern Portfolio Theory in its many refinements governs the actions of most people in the securities markets.

Modern Portfolio Theory: Balancing Risk and Reward

Risk is the chance that events will turn out differently from what was anticipated—and includes the financial consequences that result. People are intuitively averse to increased risk unless likely compensation seems great enough to justify the increased risk. This is why investors in government savings bonds expect lower returns, for little or no risk, than do investors in common stocks, where more risk and greater return are anticipated.

Risk-reward calculations always could be stated mathematically, but it wasn't until the 1950s that this type of analysis was applied to stock markets. The theories evolving from this application came to be known, collectively, as Modern Portfolio Theory. By focusing on overall portfolio composition, or asset allocation, instead of merely on individual securities, MPT provided investors with a quantitative method for determining investments on the basis of risk-reward parameters and needs.

All of Modern Portfolio Theory is predicated on three hypotheses:

(1) Investors are rational and always seek an appropriate trade-off between risk and reward;

(2) information (about companies and stocks) is dispersed quickly and in a widespread manner so that no investor has any better information than another investor; and

(3) because investors are rational and information is discounted, the marketplace itself—and individual securities within it—is basically stable, or in equilibrium. Therefore, its pricing, inherently and at any one moment in time, is efficient. This latter hypothesis is called the "efficient market theory," and is an underpinning to the pricing mechanism of all stocks in the market and the market itself.

At this point, you might be doubting the validity of these hypotheses. We all remember, with regret, those times when our own actions clearly were not rational, motivated perhaps by greed or fear or some other nonrational factor. In this era of insider-trading indictments and convictions, it is hard to argue that no investor has any better information than another. Moreover, when the market can drop 23% on a single day, as it did on October 19, 1987, it seems almost absurd to argue that on the previous session's close everything was in equilibrium.

But the theoreticians would counter that it is the combined actions of a million investors that produced a rational trade-off between risk and reward, not the decisions of a single investor. As for insider trading, a theoretical model makes no value judgments and does not adjudicate matters of equity. In fact, the use of insider information tightens up the risk-reward trade-off, as unfair as it might be to the person without the information. Finally, as we hinted in Chapter One and will argue more fully in Chapter Seven, the events of October 1987 may have much stronger logical underpinnings than anyone realizes. Keep in mind that we are talking about new ways to think about the market. Like the popular market forecaster, the market theoretician can produce a new reality (that is, a rendering of how the market actually works) by thinking about it from new and differing perspectives.

The first hypothesis of MPT—the assertion of a rational trade-off between risk and return—requires an understanding of what is called "the curve of indifference," which links the level of risk and expected reward for an equity (or for an entire portfolio) as a single point in a curve. If one then further plots out similar intersection points for that equity or portfolio, at which greater or less risk coincides with greater or less return, one establishes a series of these intersecting points. These, when drawn out, become the "curve of indifference."

In Figure Three, for example, the horizontal axis represents the measurement of risk for a specific portfolio. Risk here is defined as the percentage standard deviation of return. Standard deviation is the likelihood that an actual return will diverge from an expected return. In other words, one might expect a 10 percent return on investment plus or minus an additional amount. The standard deviation measures how big that plus or minus is.

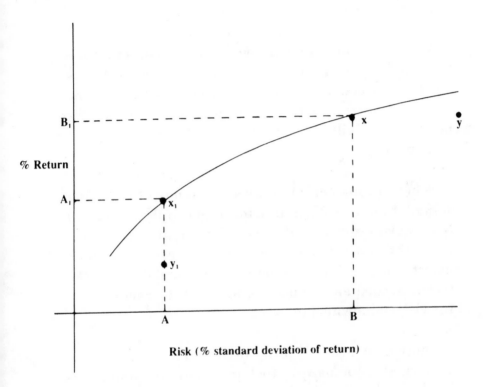

Figure Three. Risk–Reward Curve of Indifference

The vertical axis represents percentage return on investment. Return A1 is associated with taking Risk A. Return B1, a greater return, associated with Risk B, is deemed to be a fair trade-off from the combination of Return A1 and Risk A. Position X on this graph is always preferable to position Y, for instance, because, by assuming position Y, one garners only the same return while taking more risk. Point X1 is preferable to Y1, because Y1 would produce less return but at the same risk.

The curve illustrated in Figure Three represents one investor's preference. Modern Portfolio Theory relates expected reward-for-degree-of-risk to the investor's own preference concerning how much risk he or she is willing to assume for different levels of return.

When fundamental analysts attempt to predict return based on earnings forecasts and changes in price-earnings ratios, they're solving half of the equation. But how can one assess risk? In terms of a stock investment, you want to be able to calculate the risks facing a company's business in order to decide what the risk is of owning its stock.

One corollary to Modern Portfolio Theory is that the pattern of a company's stock price reveals, inductively, the health of its business. In other words, the stock-price pattern already reflects very efficiently all the information that exists concerning the fundamental value of the security. This is called the "Efficient Market Hypothesis," and it echoes the technician's view that all that is known about a stock is reflected in its price. Therefore, price itself is something we can look to for a measurement of risk: the more risky a company's business, the more likely the company's stock price is to jump around. Telephone stocks produce pretty steady financial results and so we see little fluctuation in their stock price. Small technology companies face considerable business risks, and their stock prices can fluctuate wildly. Standard deviation measures the extent of that fluctuation.

A "quick and dirty" way of comparing one stock's volatility with another's is by using a mathematical technique called *regression analysis*. Regression analysis simply plots the closing price of the market along with the closing price of an individual stock. This produces a beta coefficient, called simply a stock's "beta," and is a statistical number for relating the price movements of a stock to the price movements of the entire stock market.

By definition, the beta of the entire stock market, as represented by the S&P 500, is the whole number 1. If a particular stock moved, historically, in the exact same pattern—both up and down—as the market, then its beta would also be 1. If, however, the stock moved up and down with swings greater than the market, it would be more volatile and would have a higher beta. A high-risk stock has a high beta; a low-risk stock a low beta. If, say, a stock historically moves 11 percent up while the market moves up 10, then that stock is said to have an historical beta of 1.1. Conversely, if the stock moves only 9 percent while the market moves 10, its beta is 0.9.

Beta is symmetrical. A stock with a beta of 1.1 will fall 10 percent faster on a down market and will rise 10 percent faster in an up market; while a stock with a beta of 0.9 will retain more of its price in a down market. The latter stock is less risky than the market.

A beta number need not be assigned to merely one stock. If the entire market can have one beta number, then, obviously, an aggregate of any number of stocks—three stocks, or sixteen, or two hundred—also can have one beta assigned on the basis of how the group, in the aggregate, performs in relation to the total market.

Modern Portfolio Theory prompts the analyst or investor to focus on the composition of an entire portfolio. In constructing a portfolio that will generate a desired return for a desired risk, the portfolio manager must select from a universe of stocks. How will that selection be made? MPT advises that each selection be made in terms of the effect that that particular stock has on the already existing swings within the portfolio. A portfolio with a risk swing of plus or minus 4 percent would be less desirable than one with a swing of plus or minus 2 percent, even if both yielded an expected return of 10 percent.

The objective, always, is to minimize the volatility of the total portfolio. This means that a stock's suitability for the portfolio depends on how it "plays with" the others, the ultimate goal being to minimize risk while receiving the same return. Therefore, in assessing the interplay of varying stocks' risk-return ratios to each other, one looks for a difference in the behavior or patterns of the stocks. The manager seeks stocks that will not fluctuate the same way at the same time, in income and price, but rather ones that will fluctuate differently, thus generating less volatility in the return of the total portfolio. If stocks have a pattern of moving up and down together, they are said to have "positive covariance," and a portfolio comprising such stocks would have even more exaggerated swings. Stocks that don't swing together have "negative covariance," and a portfolio of those stocks is apt to stay a steadier course.

One would have to have incredible mathematical powers to be able to determine how every stock could be combined with every other stock at differing risk-return levels. Beta simplifies this task by substituting, within a portfolio, each's stock's relationship to the market as a definition of each stock's relationship with every other stock in the portfolio. By taking the beta of each stock and weighing it (multiplying it) according to the percentage of the portfolio that that stock occupies, you can derive a beta for the whole portfolio. This beta tells the manager how much risk his or her portfolio is taking.

Even the less sophisticated investor can calculate the apparent riskiness of his or her portfolio. Many services provide beta values for most stocks; Value Line is one example. If, after making the calculation suggested above, the investor is concerned about the potential for swings existing in the portfolio, he or she would do well to search for low-beta stocks to balance the portfolio. Conversely, the investor who is not taking enough risk would look for high-beta stocks.

The "Indifferent" Investor

Modern Portfolio Theory allows investors to construct portfolios that will usually behave in predictable ways in the aggregate even though any one stock might not. It leads people to think in terms of the entire market and portfolios (collections of stocks) rather than individual stocks. Inevitably, as investors began to think of buying groups of stocks rather than individual stocks, the notion of the "composite asset"—a collection of similar assets, like stocks, that could be viewed and handled as a single entity—emerged. The thought that equity, like debt, is *fungible* (one part may be substituted for another) gained credence. "Your stock is just like any other stock with the same beta" became an acceptable viewpoint.

To say that equity is fungible, that the stock of any company is interchangeable with the stock of any other company, may take some getting used to. Accepting the idea that debt is fungible, however, is less difficult. Debt affords a specific return based on the perceived risk of the issuer. Swapping the bonds of one similarly rated issue for the bonds of another usually causes no more comment than moving funds from one money-market account to another.

The equity of any company, viewed through the Modern Portfolio Theory risk-reward lens, is as interchangeable with the equity of any other company as are certificates of deposit issued by banks. Certainly, one company is not like any other. But the investor who thus approaches all investment with an eye only to the risk-reward equation is indifferent to other factors. The details about particular corporations or industries that often entangle investors who become enamored of stock, an industry, or a portfolio for whatever personal reasons do not trap the rational Modern Portfolio Theory investor.

One can readily swap the equity of one company for the equity of another for the same risk-adjusted return. One can also swap an entire portfolio for another portfolio composed of different equities but having the same aggregate risk and level of return, to yield the same risk-adjusted return. Further, one can swap, at a single stroke, large collections of stocks for other large collections of stocks, or entire portfolios or portions of portfolios called "baskets" for portions or baskets of stocks. This brings us, then, to a definition: a **program trade** is *the sale or purchase of a large group of stocks, a portfolio, or a basket as a single transaction.*

Asset Allocation

Equity is far from being the only asset in which portfolio managers or individuals invest. Intuitively, people know what Cervantes wrote: " 'Tis the part of a wise man to keep himself today for tomorrow, and not venture all his eggs in one basket." In the stock market, investors have interpreted this admonition to mean diversification: the wisdom of spreading one's

45

money around several stocks. Modern Portfolio Theory carries the principle further to include *asset allocation*, a mathematical method of deciding what portion of one's total resources should be allocated to various types of assets. This is a dynamic equation. The appropriate allocations will change with time and circumstances.

At the professional level, fund managers generally consider three major classes of assets: stocks, bonds or debt, and cash or cash equivalents. Within these exist such subclasses as foreign stock, growth stocks, intermediate bonds (government or corporate), and high-yield bonds. The objective of asset allocation is to increase return on assets while decreasing risk. Modern Portfolio Theory is again central to the determination of asset allocation.

Consider a portfolio consisting of Treasury bills, government bonds, and a diversified list of common stocks. Treasury bills (T-bills) are a risk-free investment; they earn a certain return and mature at the end of a stated time period (either three months, six months or one year). They are cash equivalents (and are used synonymously with the word "cash" in stock market parlance) which provide a current return with no risk of failure, default, or change in capital value. Though there is always the possibility of slight price changes over time, the short period for which one holds a T-bill virtually guarantees low volatility. (The data for T-bills here was based on T-bills with one month left before maturity. Judged on that short a time period, they truly are the same as cash.)

From 1926 to 1988, the arithmetic mean annual return from T-bills was 3.6 percent. For common stocks, return—the sum of dividends and appreciation in price—was 12.1 percent; and for bonds, return was 4.7 percent for that same period.

Risk for the three asset classes also varies. From 1926 to 1988, for stocks, risk was 20.9 percent (percentage standard deviation of annual return); for bonds, it was 8.5 percent; and for T-bills, 3.3 percent.[1] It is clear, then, that common stocks provide higher returns than do T-bills but carry greater risk; and that government bonds fall in the middle, with less risk than stocks but greater risk than T-bills, less return than stocks but greater return than T-bills.

Stocks are the riskiest investment but offer the greatest return. In most years since 1925, the return was more than the average of 12 percent; in many, it was less; and in some years, return was negative. The worst year was 1931, at minus 43.3 percent total return, while the best was 1933, at plus 54 percent. In 1954, the return was almost as good: plus 52.6 percent. By contrast, wildly swinging 1987 turned in a ho-hum performance at plus 5.2 percent.

All this says that if the normal expected return for any year is 12.0 percent, the probability is about 67 percent that the actual return will lie between plus 33

---

[1] The source for these figures is *SBBI (Stocks, Bonds, Bills and Inflation) 1988 Yearbook* (Chicago: Ibbotson Associates, 1988) *passim* plus SBBI's continuously updated reports.

percent and minus 9 percent. Here we add the standard deviation of 21 percent to the 12 percent, to arrive at 33 percent on the one side; we also subtract 21 percent from 12 percent—answer minus 9 percent—to find the other end of the range. What we are saying here is that if the past is any indication of the future, we have about a two-out-of-three possibility that the performance of the stock market will range from minus 9 percent to plus 33 percent.

It should be noted that the past includes world wars, depressions, periods of double-digit inflation, and other distinguishing features of the 1925–1988 period. The next sixty-three years will no doubt see their share of war and economic disruption. And none of this means that the next twelve months might not be completely different from what went before. But we are speaking of "probability." The risk that the market's return will lie between plus 54 percent and minus 30 percent is approximately 95 percent; and the risk that it will fall between plus 75 percent and minus 51 percent exceeds 99 percent. Put another way, the odds are 99 to 1 that in any given year, the S&P 500 will return at least minus 51 percent but not more than plus 75 percent.

The investor in stocks can shoot for even higher returns by leveraging, that is buying the stocks on margin. Current rules set by the Federal Reserve Board allow one to buy two dollars worth of stock for every one dollar put up. The other dollar would be borrowed. Essentially, then, such an investor would be 200 percent invested in the stock portfolio, by virtue of having leveraged up two-to-one. Leverage magnifies the gain or loss in the asset, in this case by a factor of two. If the market were to gain 12 percent, for instance, this leveraged investor would gain 24 percent (less borrowing and transaction costs) on the original investment. However, if the market were to drop 20 percent, this investor would be down by 40 percent.

How, then, should a sample portfolio be divided among stocks, bonds, and T-bills? The answer lies in another question: How much are investors willing to lose in order to gain? If they insist on no loss (that is, if their risk preference is zero) they will invest only in T-bills. Investors willing to accept a total rate of return that is less than what stocks alone *might* yield, in hopes of a better return than what T-bills alone *will* yield, might allocate half their assets to T-bills and the other half to stocks.

Assume that, as investors, we are willing to accept a level of risk that corresponds to standard deviation of 10.5 percent. Remember risk is the chance that events will turn out differently from what was anticipated and standard deviation is the statistic that measures just how different events might get. Choosing 10.5 percent means that one wants a two-out-of-three chance that whatever return is generated by the chosen mixture of stocks, bonds, and T-bills will vary by no more than 10.5 percent.

To reiterate, we have three asset classes with certain expected returns, certain volatility features (i.e., standard deviation) and certain relationships to each other.

Table Two

	Expected Return	Standard Deviation	Cross Correlation		
			Stocks	Bonds	T-Bills
Stocks	12.0%	21.1%	100%	11%	(7)%
Bonds	4.6%	8.5%	11%	100%	21%
T-Bills	3.5%	3.4%	(7)%	21%	100%

SOURCE: Data derived from SBBI (Stocks, Bonds, Bills and Inflation) 1988 Yearbook (Chicago: Ibbotson Associates, 1988) p. 25.

Our stated goal is to have the best portfolio within our risk parameters. What mix should be put together in order to get the maximum return at that risk point? There is some specific mix of the three asset types, with a risk level of 10.5 percent, that will produce the maximum return. There are other mixes that also have a risk of 10.5 percent but will fall short of producing the maximum return. Also, when the expected return is found it can be seen that other mixtures would have produced the same return, but would have a higher standard deviation (involved more risk).

What happens next involves a lot of complicated mathematics generally referred to as optimization analysis.[2] It isn't necessary to understand the mathematics; all one needs to know is that such mathematics exist. Take comfort; few professional investors understand the mathematics. Personal computers make optimization technique available to everyone.

Using these techniques and methods, our optimal portfolio mix would be:

Table Three

	Mix
Stocks	47.4%
Bonds	26.0%
T-Bills	26.5%
Standard Deviation 10.5%	
Expected Return 7.8%	

Figure 4 illustrates a hypothetical asset allocation mix. For each risk point along the horizontal axis, we can calculate the maximum return that can result from a mix of the three assets—stocks, bonds, and T-bills—and we can determine what that mix is. The connecting points form a curve that is called the "efficient frontier." It relates maximum return available at each risk level,

---

[2] Optimization analysis is the work of William F. Sharpe in his book *AAT Asset Allocation Tools*, Second Edition (Redwood City, California; The Scientific Press, 1987).

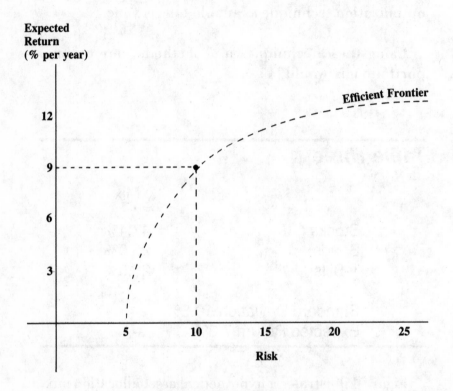

Figure Four. Asset Allocation Risk Return for 3-Asset Mix: Stocks, Bonds, & T-Bills

each point on the curve corresponding to a particular mix.

But the efficient frontier only guides us towards constructing a particular asset mix once we have already decided *what risk we will tolerate for what return*. Step one is to determine what level of risk one is satisfied with. This will vary, depending upon one's obligations.

The sponsor of a pension fund has taken on the liability of making future retirement payments to employees; the fund must earn a certain return to meet those obligations. Let's say that minimum return is 8%. Achieving that minimum return may require the sponsor to accept a higher level of risk than would otherwise be desired. If return must be 8%, we now want to know what mix will produce 8% at the lowest possible risk. For a return that is thus "pinned," there is a range of risk available. By a known algebraic equation that at first glance appears complex but, in reality, is quite calculable, one can determine both asset-mix and degree of risk for the 8% minimum return requirement.

Thanks to Modern Portfolio Theory, and the asset-allocation strategies that it has spawned, today's intelligent investor thinks more in terms of groupings of stocks and less in the old-fashioned terms of knowing whatever one can (and it was not very much in the way of a guarantee of outcome) about particular stocks.

There's no right or wrong about some of the inputs that one investor or manager will put into the computer; they will all depend on certain subjective decisions already made. Once the level of risk one is willing to accept has been determined, the components of the investment decision will be assumptions of:

(1) what the returns will be for individual assets,

(2) what the volatility of results for individual assets might be, and,

(3) how the asset classes interplay with one another within a portfolio.

There is nothing about MPT, or statistical analysis, that tells you for sure what tomorrow will bring. While certain asset classes (like T-bills) show some evidence of behaving tomorrow as they behaved yesterday, others (particularly common stocks) show no relationship between yesterday's price performance and tomorrow's price performance. In statistical terms, we use a method called serial correlation to test such statements (about the relationship of present to past) about asset classes. The historical figures on returns for different assets cited earlier in this chapter—for example, that stocks have had an average annual return of 12%—may be valid numbers to use today for very long-range forecasts. But the time-horizons of most investors, including professionals, are shorter. Thus, one still is left with the fundamental need to figure out how to forecast returns for the *appropriate* time period.

There are no secret formulae for forecasting in the computers that run the algorithms of Modern Portfolio Theory. What is also important for the investor to understand is that professional managers, once they have inserted their return forecasts and volatility forecasts into the computers, are then confronted with the need to rearrange proportions (of asset classes) within their portfolios. This process, too, causes a shift in thinking away from particular stocks and to groups of stocks. It has had a profound effect on investment decision-making.

Choosing Among Classes of Investments

Professionals managing portfolios generally confine their assets to financial instruments: stocks, bonds, and cash. Individuals need not do this. One can expand the list of classes of assets to include one's residence or investment real estate, precious metals, foreign securities, and commodities. Certain nonfinancial assets that have historically increased in value such as real estate, coins, stamps, art, collectibles, and antiques could also be included. Making the choice as to which and how many of these classes will be included in one's portfolio is asset allocation.

The reason for asset allocation is the same as for diversification—to protect and enhance the value of assets. The value of diversification exists in the probability that, at the very moment that one asset—for example the stock market—is heading downward, another asset will be appreciating in value. For example, while it can be shown that common stocks are a good hedge against inflation over the long run, it has been demonstrated that sudden sharp rises in inflation and the economic uncertainty associated with those periods can hurt the stock market significantly in the

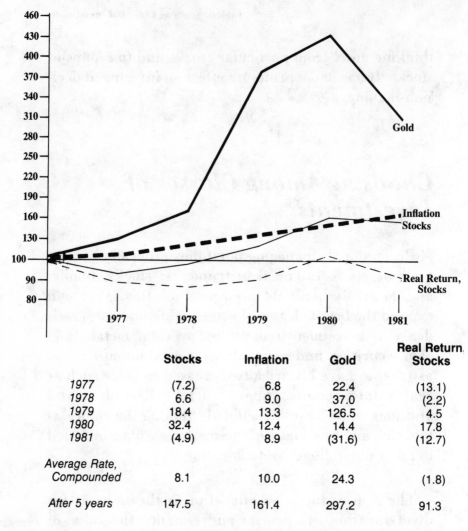

	Stocks	Inflation	Gold	Real Return, Stocks
1977	(7.2)	6.8	22.4	(13.1)
1978	6.6	9.0	37.0	(2.2)
1979	18.4	13.3	126.5	4.5
1980	32.4	12.4	14.4	17.8
1981	(4.9)	8.9	(31.6)	(12.7)
Average Rate, Compounded	8.1	10.0	24.3	(1.8)
After 5 years	147.5	161.4	297.2	91.3

Figure Five

short run. As Figure Five shows, the years 1977-1981 were a period of high inflation, and the stock market acted very poorly. But during the same period, precious metals such gold and silver showed large price increases. One would say that for that period, gold had negative covariance with stocks.

56

The algorithms that professional investors use for dynamic asset allocation require large computers. For example, Professor William Sharpe of Stanford University Graduate School of Business developed *Asset Allocation Tools (AAT)*, software described as "a Lotus 1-2-3 based portfolio optimizing package." It can be bought by anyone for several thousand dollars. *AAT* provides relevant data bases, the data from which can be manipulated to compute historic risk, returns, and correlations. One then can determine optimal portfolios for a variety of risk levels. *AAT* allows the program operator to change elements like return parameters so as to be able to construct new optimal portfolios in light of updated forecasts. Many programs exist to help private investors with access to personal computers.

Indexes and Their Derivatives

An index is a mathematical instrument that attempts to define the behavior of an entire class of assets by taking the average of a few members of the class. It is important to understand that an index is only a number. Unlike the items that comprise it, an index has no concrete reality. One usually sets the first calculation of the index's time sequence at an easy-to-remember number like 10 or 100, so that one can relate changes in the index to this base level. With computers and electronic access to current price data, it is feasible today to track all members of a class, and thus to compute the value of the entire stock market. The Wilshire 5000 Index is as complete a calculation of the entire stock market as exists. However, the Dow Jones Index, consisting of only 30 stocks, remains the most popular index; and the S&P 500 Index remains the most widely used base against which to measure investment performance. Professional money managers, when they send you reports on your account, will tell you how your account performed relative to the S&P 500. The indexes remain in use because they are convenient, because they provide a historical record, because investment products based on them now exist and, not least, because they are good marketing tools for such sponsors as Dow Jones, Standard & Poor's, Value Line, Wilshire Associates, and others.

Types of Indexes

The Wall Street Journal and other publications list several widely used and followed indexes. Each tries to measure and track activity in its entire market.

The best-known stock market index is the Dow Jones Industrial Average (DJIA). When people say, "the market's up" or "the market's down," they usually mean that the DJIA is up or down. The Dow comprises only 30 stocks, but its component securities are by no means a constant. Entire industries as well as corporations fall out of favor or emerge; as a result, companies are dropped from the index or added to it. As corporations issue stock, split the stock, merge, or go out of business, index divisors, multipliers and weightings are changed. These adjustments are an attempt to assure continuity, so that when the index is at 2,000, it really is twice as high as it was at 1,000.

Also in the Dow Jones group are the Dow Jones Transportation Index (20 stocks), the Dow Jones Utilities Index (15 stocks), and Dow Jones Composite Index of 65 stocks, which encompasses all three indexes. The transportation and industrial indexes are the heart of Dow Theory; their relative movements with regard to one another are believed by some, but not by us, to herald major movements in the stock market and the economy.

Among the other indexes are:

(1) The New York Stock Exchange Composite, which includes over 1400 Industrials, Transportation, Utilities, and Finance;

(2) Standard & Poor's 500, which incorporates S&P's 400 Industrials, 20 Transportation, 40 Utilities, and 40 Financials. The market value of these firms matches about 80 percent of the total market value of all companies on the New York Stock Exchange. A popular subset of the S&P 500 is the S&P 100;

(3) The Amex Index which covers all stocks on the American Stock Exchange;

(4) The Major Market Index, containing 20 large-capitalization stocks. The index was designed in 1983 by the American Stock Exchange to replicate the Dow Jones Index and to provide a basis for trading options and futures based on an index similar to the Dow Jones;

(5) The Value Line Composite Index, which reflects the value of some 1,685 stocks followed by the Value Line investment advisory service of Arnold Bernhard & Company. These stocks account for about 95 percent of total dollar equity trades in the U.S.;

(6) The Over-the-Counter (OTC) market, now largely computerized, on the National Association of Securities Dealers Automated Quotations (NASDAQ) system, which has the OTC index and the corresponding industrials, insurance, and financial stocks as well as the National Market Industrials; and

(7) The Russel 2000 and 3000 and the Wilshire Associates Equity 5000, which are based on, respectively, 2,000, 3,000, and 5,000 securities and are thus the broadest indexes. The Wilshire isn't really an index; it is the total dollar value of all the shares of the 5,000 stocks multiplied by their price, for the total capitalization of the stocks. It is usually expressed without the $ sign or the last six digits. The Wilshire closed in 1987 at $2.417123 trillion, down $17.826 billion from its 1986 close.

None of these indexes is actually a simple arithmetic average of the prices of the stocks in the index, though some, like the Dow Jones, started that way. The average price of a security listed on the New York Stock Exchange, for example, is well under $100; on March 31, 1988, it was $20.90. But the NYSE Composite Index currently runs between 150 and 200, the DJIA exceeds 2,000, and the S&P 500 is over 250.

Components of an Index

Originally, the usefulness of an index was its value as a sample. If one could not compute all relevant information about every stock in the stock market, it was useful to have a sample of stocks, whose information could be known, that accurately represented the entire market. Today, however, computer technology makes it possible to collect and store information about every single stock in the market. So why retain indexes? The answer seems to be because they now have a validity and credibility of their own, even when they no longer earn it, based simply on the historical acceptance of their value. Thus indexes *are* important, and tender loving care is given to their makeup. If a company drops out of the Dow, for example, because of merger, great care is given to choosing its replacement.[3] Even the S&P 500, which includes 500 stocks (but not *all* stocks) must select replacements carefully in order to ensure its long-range value.

Though no longer essential as a sample of the market in informational terms, the S&P 500 does have value both as a yardstick for measuring portfolio performance and as a blueprint that indexers replicate. It is worth repeating, however, that all this is only because we are boxed in by an antiquated system that continues

---

[3] 1987 changes in components of the Dow included The Coca-Cola Company's replacement of Owens-Illinois, Inc.; The Boeing Company's replacement of Inco Ltd.; and American Can Company's name-change to Primerica Corp.

to value the Dow and other indexes long after their usefulness has expired.

While the character of an index reflects its components, the utility of the index does not depend on any one component. Indexes endure as distinct entities though their components may change. An index that is a closed compilation of certain stocks that go on forever soon would not represent the market it purports to index. The market of securities in real-world industries and corporations would operate independently of the index, and it would lose its usefulness to investors. For this reason, indexes constantly must be updated both as to the selection of components and with arithmetic technical adjustments that reflect what is happening to the components.

The index committees have developed formulas that apply a variety of weighting factors, which themselves change with time and circumstances, to ensure continuity in the index value. Stock splits, changes in capitalization, dividend declarations, and other events affecting an individual stock, which could cause the figure to fluctuate from internal causes if factored into the average without adjustment, are calculated into a divisor that adjusts the index to compensate for the event.

If the stock of a constituent company splits 2 for 1, for example, the price of the stock will be half what it was. In an index comprising only 30 stocks (the DJIA) or 20 stocks (the Major Market Index), such a drop in share price would cause a precipitous decline in the index. So the formula adjusts a divisor to account for the split. The index then shows only the change in total capitalization resulting from market forces.

But even that calculation is not as simple as it seems. In a *price-weighted index*, which is a simple average of the prices of the stocks divided first by the number of stocks and then by the divisor for continuity, the weight swing in the index by a company whose stock has split 2 for 1 will be half what it was.

Consider, for example, three stocks, A, B, and C, priced, respectively, at 80, 90, and 100. Their sum is 270. We will designate the divisor as 3 and thus the index is 90; in other words, 270 divided by three. Stock A splits 2 for 1; the new price is 40. The sum of the three stocks is now 230. For the index to remain at 90, we must divide 230 by a new divisor so that our index will have continuity with the old one. The new divisor becomes 2.555, or 230 divided by 2.555, equaling 90.

Let's assume our new $40 stock goes to $44, equivalent to $88 on the old stock before the split. The increase in stock A's old shares would have bumped the index to 92.6667, up by 2.96 percent. After the split, however, A's influence is reduced, despite the divisor, and the increase bumps the index to 91.5636, up by only 1.74 percent.

Such an effect is neither infrequent nor trivial. It can raise havoc with portfolio managers whose positions are tied to the index; it also may have an impact on the relationship between the index and its derivative products. To program traders, the composition and continuity of the indexes mean much more than simply a way to track the market.

Index funds should mirror the index in their holdings. An index fund manager buys shares of each stock in the exact proportion that exists in the index. But when an index changes its composition through shifts in actual issues (or through alterations in existing ones that affect the weighting), the fund, in turn, must buy or sell stocks to restore its mirror image. The effects of such a change in an index may have been dramatically demonstrated on April 14, 1988, when the DJIA fell 101 points for its fifth worst loss ever.

On the evening of April 13, the Standard & Poor's 500 index committee removed three stocks from the 500 and replaced them with three others. The deleted companies had a total capitalization of $600 million; the capitalization of their replacements was $11.8 billion. The change required adjustment to the weightings of all stocks in the index so that the index number at the opening of the market on April 14 would be the same as at the close on the 13th. That adjustment forced index fund managers to reposition their portfolios to match the new composition of the index, which they could do only by selling some stocks and buying others. These funds were said to have sold significant quantities of the largest capitalization issues that also comprise the Dow Jones index. That selling activity, according to the theory, helped drop the Dow nearly 50 points more than it would have fallen on other news that same day.

Like private clubs, the indexes differ not only in numbers but also in the manner in which they choose members. The selection gives each index a different bias, making each more representative of one sector of the total market than another.

Another factor that contributes to the usefulness of an index in a particular circumstance is the type of weighting it employs. The simplest index, as mentioned earlier, is a price-weighted one. All one needs to do is to add up the prices of the component stocks and divide the result by the number of stocks to arrive at an average price for all the stocks. However, as noted in the preceding example of the effects of stocks splits, the price-weighting method introduces problems of its own. A high-priced stock with few shares outstanding will affect the index much more than a low-price stock with many shares outstanding. Both the DJIA and the Major Market Index are price-weighted. Since their components are also large-capitalization "blue chip" stocks, these two indexes do not accurately reflect activity in smaller companies.

Capitalization-weighted indexes are calculated in the same manner as price-weighted ones except that the individual issues affect, or weight, the index in proportion to their total capitalization. Capitalization equals the number of shares outstanding multiplied by the price of each share. In such indexes, which include the Standard & Poor's 500 and the New York Stock Exchange Composite, big companies with low stock prices swing more weight than small companies with high stock prices. Stock splits have no effect, though other changes in capitalizations that change the numbers of shares outstanding, such as the sale of more stock or repurchases of stock, will affect the weighting.

Another type of index, designed to remedy the imperfections of the first two, is the geometric average index, or equal-dollar index. Such an index, of which the Value Line Composite Index is the exemplar, looks only to the percentage change in a stock price without regard either to its price or its capitalization. It assumes $100 invested in each stock in the index. To calculate this index, one takes the percentage change in the prices of each component stock, multiplies them together, then takes the nth root of the product, n being equal to the number of stocks in the index.

Consider 20 stocks, priced at $1 increments from $1 to $20. The arithmetic average, or index, for this group is 10.5.

$$\frac{(1+2+3+4+5+6+7+8+9+10+11 + 12+13+14+15+16+17+18+19+20)}{20} = 10.5$$

We can multiply by 9.5238 to make it 100. The geometric average, based on percentage and by definition, is 100, since it assumes $100 invested in each stock, for a total of $2,000 divided by 20.

If each stock increases in price by 10 percent, the range of increases for the arithmetic average will be from 10 cents to two dollars The new prices will range from \$1.20 to \$22.00. The new arithmetic average will be 11.55 (9.5 × 1.1); the index will be 110 (100 × 1.1). The geometric average, however, will increase by the nth root of the product of the new prices, that is, the twentieth root of $1.1 \times 2.2 \times 3.3 \ldots \times 22$, or 26.783×10^{18}, which is 9.36252. The new index will be not 110 but 109.36.

The geometric index easily accommodates stock splits. Percentages are adjusted to the post-split price. But as the example shows, the index has a built-in bent. The geometric average will always be slightly lower than the arithmetic average of the same items. Since the average value of any real stock portfolio will always be an arithmetic average (add up the prices of all the securities, divide by the number of shares, and arrive at an arithmetic average value per share), a geometric average presents problems to arbitrageurs and index fund managers. It's more difficult to relate the index to the actual prices of the underlying stocks.

This peculiarity of the geometric index has led Value Line to switch to an arithmetic index. The new index, introduced in March 1988, is also equal-dollar weighted—it assumes \$1 invested in each stock. But the index is a simple arithmetic average in which the day-to-day change is expressed as a percentage of the previous day's close. The entire portfolio is re-balanced once daily, while the geometric index is re-balanced continuously. The first futures contract based on the arithmetic average closed in September 1988, while the June 1988 contract was the last on the geometric index.

When a stock pays a dividend, its price for that day reflects the payment by falling an amount equal to the dividend. The stock is said to be *ex-dividend*. The price hasn't changed as far as investors are concerned, because they have both the dividend and the stock. The total value of the asset remains the same. But the price has fallen. And since the indexes recognize only price, the indexes also fall. For investors in the securities themselves, the effect is minimal. However, for investors in the instruments based on the indexes (index futures, index options, and options on index futures) the index decline is important.

Dividend payments are related in indexes as price declines, but the effects are not uniform over time because companies tend to go ex-dividend in the second month of the quarter. Investors in index futures and options can benefit by monitoring these dividend-induced declines in the indexes.

From Indexes to Indexing

Indexing is the active process of investing in indexes. And the S&P 500 is the index usually used. In the early 1970s, the case for indexing became compelling. If the market is efficient and in equilibrium as Modern Portfolio Theory shows it to be, why should any investor spend time and money trying to outperform it? Our answer is clearly that one should not. Yet there are explanations for why many investors and portfolio managers are slow to accept the answer.

One explanation can be found in the contagious notion that hope springs eternal, even when facts prove otherwise. This is why people bet on horses, roulette wheels and lotteries; and it is why and how some people buy stocks. In October 1987, while 1,973 New York Stock Exchange issues dropped, and 1,068 of them hit new lows, 52 stocks gained and 10 of those actually reached new highs for the year. Those stocks beat the averages on that day, and somewhere out there watching the event was an investor (or investors) who read the lesson as, "See, you *can* do better than the market by picking the right stocks." The fact is that the probability is quite high that you can't.

Yet most investors, large and small, strive to beat the averages. Averages are, after all, averages: some of the items within them will go up and some will go down; some will change at differing rates and at differing times. Since the averages are indexes that represent much larger groupings than their components, intuition tells many people that it should be possible to identify in the total market those securities that consistently perform better than the averages on indexes. It isn't, but the hope persists.

Some market approaches turn in better-than-index performance for some time—long enough for their proponents to believe they have found a way to beat the market forever. Depending on the investor's own time horizon, "forever" may be six months or a year, and the validity of the techniques over time is viewed as irrelevant. Some of the severe beatings taken in October 1987 were taken by highly regarded stock-picking strategies that had produced good results for years.

From time to time, individual funds may perform better on average than the market averages. But even over a relatively short period, no large fund consistently does better. In the bull market of 1987, through August, 85 percent of professional money managers failed to match the performance of the S&P 500 index. Over the longer term, the S&P 500 consistently has outperformed between 60 percent and 70 percent of professional money managers.

Why do money managers generally do worse than the market? Partly because they continually try to do better. Their attempts require them to spend money on research, to sell stocks that disappoint and buy new ones to replace them, and to pay salaries and incentives to advisers and managers.

Thus, even if the stocks in the fund do perform as well as the market averages, the fund must then deduct costs of transaction, research, and management.[4] The quest for consistently better performance supports an

---

[4] One might think that individual investors would have lower overhead and therefore would net more from investments. But that is not the case: Individuals have much higher transaction costs, and overall commission rates for individuals have been increasing. Individuals also have tax liabilities that many funds, particularly pension funds, do not. Individuals do incur research costs in the subscription rates to financial newspapers, magazines and advisory services. And they may well pay management fees if they employ professionals to advise and manage their investments.

enormous constituency. Further, some types of funds such as mutual funds must keep cash in their portfolios to pay shareholders who redeem their shares. Indeed, cash-short funds were one factor in the October 19, 1987, crash. Mutual fund shareholders as well as holders of individual stocks rushed to turn in their shares, which the funds had to redeem in cash. To raise cash, the funds had to sell their stock holdings, which was difficult to do at any price that Monday. The funds' huge holdings, all brought to market at one time, exerted enormous downward pressure. One fund organization alone, Fidelity of Boston, had to sell hundreds of separate stock issues with a total value upwards of a billion dollars.

But holding cash can adversely affect a fund because cash does not participate in the market and thus it skews the fund's performance. *The Wall Street Journal* noted: "During the five-year bull market, some of the best performing mutual funds were those with low levels of cash. As the market bounded ahead at a 28 percent annual rate, the 6 percent to 10 percent return on cash reserves, usually invested in Treasury bills or other short-term instruments, became a big drag on performance."[5] During the past five years, mutual funds on average held about 9 percent of their assets in cash.

Merely to match the averages, therefore, an actively managed fund must perform better than the averages. It must recover its overhead costs, the total of which

---

[5] *The Wall Street Journal*, December 18, 1987.

approximates 4.4 percent for the typical common stock mutual fund, including annual transaction costs of 3.2 percent and administrative costs, such as fees to managers and advisors, averaging 1.2 percent. To this one must add the cash drag in the portfolio, as noted above.

The search for better-than-market performance also belies its own assertions. If it were true that certain strategies were more successful at identifying stocks or groups of stocks that consistently were better performers, those strategies soon would be discounted. As the information was quickly dispersed throughout the marketplace, *all* investors would begin using those strategies, which soon would render them nothing more than just another factor in overall market performance. Equilibrium and the efficient market would continue as before. "The traditional valuation strategies have simply become too popular to be of much use," is how *The Wall Street Journal* accounted for the failure of well-known stock picking strategies in 1987.[6]

The reality of today's market is that the bulk of investment is made by large funds and portfolio managers, which is why any action or strategy that becomes widespread has large and near-immediate consequences for market price-shifts. In 1987, these institutional investors—which include mutual funds, pension plans, profit-sharing plans and insurance funds—accounted for 51.2 percent of all shares traded on the New York Stock Exchange.

---

[6] *The Wall Street Journal*, September 15, 1987, p. 35.

These managers are hard-pressed to find sufficient areas of opportunity in which to invest their multibillion-dollar funds before their own actions have great affect on those areas. They can't make a move without affecting the market. Thus, though the research managers of such funds are seeking bargain stocks even more assiduously than do amateur investors, the amount they can effectively invest in those situations is limited.

The size of the institutional funds has other ramifications for investment: In order not to cause wide fluctuations in the market, the bulk of investments will be in large-capitalization companies, which means primarily the blue-chip stocks that make up the S&P 500. You now can begin to see the logical outcome (or what *should* be the logical outcome) of these factors. If institutional investors, because of limitations in their flexibility, are going to wind up investing in primarily S&P stocks—that is, a broad representation of the market—why not simply buy the index at the start?

Index Funds

The overwhelming evidence is that it is impossible for a large fund with many investments to perform consistently better than the market over a significant period. If such a fund did do better than the market, the performance was an aberration, not a norm. If you cannot consistently beat the averages and are likely to do worse two out of three times despite your best efforts, why not construct a fund whose portfolio consists only of stocks in the indexes and with the same weighting as they have in the index?

The arguments against such a strategy were and are mainly subjective. Fund managers are paid to make their funds perform better than the market as a whole. If fund managers need do no more than buy stocks that are in the averages—in effect, abdicate their function to whatever committee decides the composition of an index—then they may be thought of as taking money under false pretenses. Anyone can look at the list of stocks comprising an index and buy the same stocks in the same weightings. Why should anyone pay large management fees to fund managers to do that?

Although the idea of the *index fund* had been born, managers continued to believe throughout the late 1960s and early 1970s that they could do better than the averages and strove to do so. Modern Portfolio Theory remained largely in the realm of academics and had little practical application. Active management was the order of the day and index funding was looked upon as passive management, unworthy of professionals.

In 1971, at a Harvard Business School seminar for pension fund managers, Jeremy Grantham, then of Batterymarch Investment Company, publicly introduced the idea of an index fund. Grantham said he couldn't understand why the pension fund managers didn't just hire the people who determine what stocks will be in the Standard & Poor's 500 Index. The idea was not well received by the managers nor by his boss, but Grantham continued to raise it. Meanwhile, on the West Coast, Thomas Logue and William Fouse, then of Wells Fargo Bank, entertained much the same idea.

Nothing much happened at first. The idea was talked about, but no one offered a product. Then one day a risk-averse organization that wanted to invest its funds very conservatively sought Batterymarch's help. Grantham developed an index fund portfolio. Although the client declined it, Batterymarch was then on record as having offered such a product.

By February 1976, only $500 million was invested in index funds offered by only three firms: Battery-march, Wells Fargo, and American National Bank. Index funds as a percentage of total funds under management slowly increased in number and size through the 1970s and into the 1980s. Though their numbers have exploded since the mid-1980s (the total exceeded $150 billion by mid-1988), they are still not considered respectable by many money managers and their clients, who feel that money managers should justify their fees by gains achieved through active management.

Nonetheless, the largest funds cannot avoid being index funds to some extent, given their size and the constraints they experience as a result. Jeremy Grantham speaks for many index fund managers when he notes: "The case for indexing is compelling, partly because large institutions, as a group, are a reasonable proxy for the market. If they are the market, they cannot beat themselves."[7] The financial community is becoming more comfortable with the idea as more studies indicate that there really is no other way to go.

Grantham, who now heads his own firm, Grantham, Mayo, Van Otterloo, in Boston, justifies indexing on the basis of cost as much as on the futility of trying to outguess the market. Active management costs money. *Transaction by transaction*, the securities market is a zero-sum game. When A sells 100 shares of stock to B, the sum of the transaction is zero. The participants have traded items of equal value and, at the instant of the trade, neither side gains or loses value. But commissions and fees do subtract value from each transaction. The more transactions, the more the erosion of value.

This zero-sum game differs from the classic example of a zero-sum game: poker. In poker, the sum of all transactions from start to finish of the game is zero— the amount of money in play is a constant—but the value of each player's stake changes with each hand, at every transaction. In the securities markets, the net value of each player's "hand" (the trade) is constant, but the size of the pot continually changes.

Thus the distinction "transaction by transaction" is important. The equities markets, as surrogates for the economy, are not zero-sum but constantly expand or, occasionally, contract. When one buys stock at price X and later sells it at price Z, the change in price, up or

---

[7] From an interview with Jeremy Grantham and the authors.

down, is a shift in value, not a sum subtracted from the other side of the transaction. That change in value of the individual asset contributes to the change in value of the entire "pot," the total market.

One factor continually removes money from the securities game pot—management. In every transaction where stock changes hands, the broker and the money manager get fees. "The process of management subtracts mightily from the pie," Grantham observes. Consider a poker game that has a banker (the house) who takes a fee for each hand but puts nothing back in the pot. Eventually, since the supply of money in the game does not increase, the banker will have it all unless one player cleans out all the others first.

Unlike poker, however, the securities pie continues to grow as if some benefactor (call it the economy) kept adding money to the pot while not participating in the game. "There is a long-run uptrend in most averages of stocks prices in line with the long-run growth of earnings and dividends,"[8] says Burton Malkiel in *A Random Walk Down Wall Street*. The holdings of each player, regardless of the size of each one's stake, the outcome of each hand, and the fees extracted per transaction, will increase in value as the entire pot grows, if they are prudently managed. They would increase more if no fees had to be paid.

---

[8] Burton G. Malkiel, *A Random Walk Down Wall Street*, 2nd Ed. (New York: W.W. Norton, 1981), p. 129.

Chapter Three ————————————

TOOLS OF PROGRAM TRADING: BASIC DEFINITIONS

Men and Machines

The stock exchanges today are highly automated in most of their activities. Information about changes in prices and index levels is available instantly to everyone. Even the individual investor can have up-to-the-second prices piped into his home computer over a phone line. Orders to buy and sell are transmitted around the world at the speed of light, from broker to broker. Computers provide instant confirmation of trades.

Yet humans are still very much involved in the operation of the market. On the trading floor, specialists direct trading. The actual trades are still handled one at a time by flesh and blood, pencil and paper. It is a system as old as the exchange itself. Each of the 1,500 stocks that trade on the New York exchange is assigned to one of approximately 54 specialist firms which maintain a trading post on the floor. Each firm is responsible for the trading in a list of stocks and maintains an order book into which offers to buy and sell stock are recorded. They control the synapses of the market's central nervous system, keeping unclogged and orderly the gate between transaction.

The orders are placed by brokers acting for their customers or for themselves. But it is the specialist who orchestrates the deal. He can tell from his book if the prevailing mood for a stock is positive or negative by the ratio of orders to buy to orders to sell. The market is an auction, and the specialist is the auctioneer with an important difference: He agrees to use his own capital to keep the trading action orderly and dependable in the stocks assigned to his firm. He is a businessman with an exclusive franchise: For the price of his seat on the exchange the specialist agrees to buy stock and support the price when no one else wants to. He also agrees to have stock for sale, or to sell short if he doesn't own any himself. His purpose is to ensure a more or less steady and dependable trade in his stocks. His profit comes from the thinnest of margins on a large number of very short-term trades.

Critics complain that this system is an anachronism, although the system works the way it is supposed to most of the time. They believe it is possible for machines to be trained to match buy and sell orders without human intervention. In fact, such systems have been set up, but have not proven popular. For one thing, brokers representing buyers and sellers prefer to obtain information about how a market has been trading before acting on their clients' orders. Second, person-to-person contact allows room for negotiation of terms. Third, part of the specialist's function is to provide capital for the purpose of facilitating orders. All of these would cease to exist in an exclusively computerized trading market.

The specialist system faced a severe crisis during the October 1987 crash. The wave of selling washed away approximately $200 million of specialist firms' own capital. Several were so badly wounded they had to close their doors. Others were swallowed up by stronger firms in forced marriages.

While the specialists clearly were no match for the volume unleashed by the panic, neither were the supposedly automated actors. The stock exchange's *Designated Order Turnaround* (DOT) system stopped working. DOT appears to execute trades automatically but it doesn't. The system, owned by the New York and American exchanges, transmits orders directly from brokers anywhere in the world to the specialists' trading post on the exchange floors, and almost instantly returns confirmation that the trade was made.

DOT was inaugurated in 1976, principally as a means of batching groups of small orders of 100 or so shares. The system combined dozens of small repetitive functions into single larger trades, giving specialists more time to concentrate on disposing of big blocks of stock, which require more care to avoid disrupting the market and causing wide price swings. Trading speeded up, and as the system proved itself capable, the exchanges permitted DOT to handle larger blocks. In 1977, the size for market orders (orders to be executed at the prevailing market price) was raised to 299 shares, and to 500 shares for limit orders (which are to be executed only at a specific price). By 1988, the limits had been raised to 30,099 for market orders and 99,999 for limit orders.

As the capacity of DOT grew to handle larger trades, the system became a key link and facilitator of program trading. A portfolio manager, at the touch of a button on his desk, could instantly transmit orders to buy or sell several thousand shares and get back a speedy confirmation. Programs could be executed faster, taking better advantage of temporary price discrepancies in the markets. The investment manager who needed to put into motion a major portfolio change also could transmit orders to sell a whole list of stocks simultaneously to all the different specialists who handled those stocks. Whereas individual investors are likely to add or remove stocks from their portfolios one at a time, managers of major funds will replace an entire portfolio in one action to reflect a change in investment goals or the economic outlook.

At the heart of program trading is the notion that many stocks share similar characteristics and their prices will behave similarly under certain conditions. They may be in the same business, such as electric utilities, or they may share the fact that they usually hold up well in bear markets, or that they outperform in bull markets. Whatever the similarities between them, the stocks have been chosen to build a portfolio with specific goals or to add certain qualities to a larger portfolio.

Investment professionals call these groups of stocks *baskets*. Sometimes they will sell or buy an entire basket at a time. Once he has decided that a certain group of stocks no longer fits the goals of the portfolio, or that changes in the economic scene dictate a more aggressive or more defensive investment posture, the portfolio manager will try to sell all the stocks in a basket as quickly as possible and just as quickly reinvest the money in a different basket. A basket of stocks to be bought or sold first came to be referred to as a *buy* or *sell program* in the early 1970s, even before index funds arrived on the scene.

The Advent of Stock Options

At about the same time that program trading began to grow, investment professionals were experimenting with other less clumsy ways to play the entire market. They looked for inspiration, among other places, from the *futures market*, which traditionally has been associated with commodities such as grains, livestock, metals, and oil. The principal value of the futures markets in industrial or agricultural goods is that it allows producers to nail down the cost of their raw materials ahead of time. This, in turn, allows the producer to quote profitable prices to his customers without worrying that a big swing in the cost of his raw materials will wipe him out.

Futures serve as a kind of risk insurance. A miller, for instance, contracts to buy a thousand bushels of wheat in three months at a preagreed price. If the price of wheat rises in three months time when he takes physical possession of the grain, the miller has saved himself the added cost. If the price falls instead, the miller is stuck with his expensive wheat, but that is the price of locking in the cost of his raw materials.

Not everyone who sells a wheat future is a boot-clad farmer in overalls. *Speculators* sell futures contracts on commodities without actually owning the commodities because they expect to be able to fill the contracts they make by buying in the cash market at lower prices on the day of reckoning. A trader who sells wheat futures today expects to profit from a decline in the bushel price: he hopes to be able to deliver wheat for less than he sold it months earlier. If he miscalculates, he has to buy wheat for more than he sold it and he posts a loss on the transaction.

Once a futures contract is sold, its value will fluctuate in response to the rise and fall of the underlying commodity. At any time, the miller or the investor can sell the contract to someone else, the same as a stock or a bond. Most futures contracts change hands many times and are principally traded by speculators, although, ultimately, somebody has to take possession of the commodity on the due date, whether it be a car-load of wheat or a ship full of heating oil.

Options are similar to futures except that options generally grant the right to purchase, whereas futures bestow an *obligation* to do so. Everyone has heard of options on property. Sometimes they are embedded in leases. A business may rent a building with an option to buy it by some future date, perhaps at the expiration of the lease, at a predetermined price. Or an investor or builder may take an option from a landowner to buy a piece of property he hopes to develop at a later date, perhaps after obtaining approval for his building plans from government agencies.

Sometimes these options are transferrable. The holder of the option can sell his right to purchase the building or the land to a third party without consulting the property owner who granted the option in the first place. In this event, the option acquires a worth of its own, a value derived from the value of the land or structure itself and affected by other factors such as the cost of mortgage money, demand for housing or office space, availability of water and sewer, etc.

Stock options are similar to real estate options with some obvious differences. Prices in the stock market are far more volatile, changing as they often do from trade to trade, and thus the price of stock options is equally volatile. The process of calculating the true worth of a stock option has been compared to trying to hunt down a housefly by tracking only the movements and size of its shadow. And whereas an option on real estate will always during its life retain some value (unless, of course, it turns out there's an old radium dump buried on the site), a stock option can lose all of its value by the time it expires.

An investor can buy and sell options with the same ease that the stocks themselves may be bought and sold. There are two kinds of options on stocks: one that gives the holder the right to buy the stock and one that grants the right to sell. The option to buy is a *call option*: it gives the holder the right to call the stock to himself. The option to sell is a *put option*: it gives the investor the right to put the stock into someone else's hands—to sell. In the shorthand of Wall Street, call options are simply "calls" and put options are "puts."

As in an option on real estate, the price of a stock option is predetermined at the time the option is first created. Suppose an investor owns 1,000 shares of IBM and decides to sell someone else an option to buy those shares. She checks the current market price of IBM shares and finds the stock selling at $100. She decides that the price at which she could be persuaded to let her shares go is $110. So she sells call options on her IBM shares that give someone else the right to buy 1,000 shares of that stock at $110 a share, which is called the *strike price* or the *exercise price*.

Why would anyone pay for the privilege to buy a stock at $110 a share when the stock is trading at only $100? The answer is that they wouldn't pay much. But the buyer is betting that someday soon, before the option expires, IBM will trade higher than $110 a share, and the option will then have some real value. In this instance, the buyer of 10 calls on IBM, exercisable at $110 a share, might pay 50 cents a share for that right. Because the stock is trading below the exercise price, the cost of the option is all fluff and promise and is therefore referred to as a *premium*. If the stock starts to rise, the price of the option is likely to rise with it as the possibility grows that IBM shares actually could reach $110 and maybe streak on by to higher prices. If IBM reaches $105 a share, the value of the 110 calls may double, or even triple in anticipation. If the stock price does hit $110 and keeps going, the option is said to be "in the money." In other words, it now has real value as opposed to a premium value based on hope. If the stock price rises to $115, the calls exercisable at $110 now have a real, tangible value of at least $5 a share. The options may trade at an even higher price if there is a reasonable expectation that the share price of IBM is going to keep rising. The difference between the real value, $5, and the actual price of the option is, once again, called the premium.

The holder of the options in this example can sell the calls to someone else and take her profit; she can exercise the right to buy and sell the stock in the market to take her profit; she can hold the stock to collect a dividend payment; or she can hold out for a higher price.

The investor who bought those IBM calls paid just 50 cents a share. He didn't have to ante up to buy the stock at $100 a share, so his money worked a lot harder than it could have by buying common stock. And if the price of the options rose to $5, he made a huge profit, in percentage terms, larger than he ever could have expected if he had bought the stock outright. To make the same percentage profit in the underlying shares of IBM, the price would have had to soar to $1,000 a share.

Puts work the same way, except that they increase in value as the stock falls. The owner of the same IBM shares creates an option that grants the right to sell stock to another investor at a predetermined price. The call owner wants the price of the stock to rise as much as possible. But big price moves take quite a lot of time, unless there is an unexpected positive business development or takeover bid. Or, the stock is historically subject to wide price swings that would make it likely to reach the exercise price before expiration.

Time, therefore, is the most powerful enemy of options. It gradually whittles away at the price. Calls and puts generally come on the market for the first time with expiration dates nine months away. Whereas time favors a stock (eventually, if for no other reason than inflation is likely to carry the price higher), time destroys an option. For that reason, most options are traded frequently. Investors typically hold on to them for relatively short periods of time before deciding to take a profit or limit a loss. Option prices will sometimes drop between Friday's close and Monday's opening for no apparent reason except that some investors realized over the weekend that their calls or puts were one week closer to expiring.

Calls are more popular than puts in the same way that it is more popular to buy and own stocks than it is to sell stocks short. Most options are bought and sold many times over before they expire, and very often they expire worthless, which is the maximum risk in the ordinary options investment.

In their purest form, calls are written and sold by people who own stock. An insurance company or a pension fund that owns stock will sell calls on that stock. The investment manager looks at his stock and decides at what price he would be willing to take a profit. He then writes and sells the calls with that strike price. If the buyer of the calls actually exercises the option to buy the stock, the investment manager has made his profit on the stock plus extra money selling the calls. He is gambling, of course, that he won't see the price of the stock going up even higher and miss out on an even larger profit. Depending on his investment goals, an investment manager might prefer to see those options expire worthless and unexercised so that he can turn around and sell a new set of calls.

On the other hand, puts are often written by people who don't own the stock and hope that the option will not be exercised under any circumstances. A put option writer places himself in the position of being obligated to buy stock at a loss. He sells, for instance, puts on IBM with a strike price of 90. The stock is trading at $100 and he gets a premium for the puts of 50 cents. If the stock never gets below $90 a share, the puts won't be exercised and the writer gets to keep the premium. But if the stock sinks to $85, the investor who bought those puts has the right to go out into the market and buy that IBM for $85 a share, then turn around and sell that same stock to the put writer for $90 a share. The put writer faces a loss of $5 a share, minus the 50 cents he got for selling the puts in the first place. Because of the nature of this transaction, you can see why puts are less popular.

There is an even riskier transaction—to write calls without actually owning the stock. Someone who writes such calls, termed *naked*, without owning stock and then sees the stock soar way above the exercise price, runs the risk that the buyer of those calls will demand delivery of the stock itself at the exercise price. In other words, if you write naked IBM 100 calls, and the stock rockets to 130, you may have to go into the market to buy IBM at $130 a share for delivery to the call owner at only $100 a share for $30-a-share loss. In theory, the potential loss in such a transaction is unlimited.

Holders of options exercise them infrequently. Most investors buy and sell them on any of the five exchanges that trade options, taking profits when they can make them. Options more typically are exercised in the last hours of the day on which they expire. Big brokerage house trading desks frequently buy call options just before they expire and then exercise them at the eleventh hour at a small profit, knowing that they have customers for the stock they will end up owning. Or they will buy puts and exercise them knowing that their firms own shares they wish to sell.

In the same way that a miller buys wheat futures to lock in the cost of his raw materials, stock market investors use options and futures as a kind of "insurance" or hedge against future price risk. Suppose an investor who owns 1,000 shares of IBM he acquired for $100 a share is worried that the stock market looks weak and that IBM might be in for a tumble. Yet, he is a long-term investor and isn't ready to sell. Perhaps there is also a dividend payment coming up that he doesn't want to miss. He could hedge himself by purchasing puts with a $95 strike price. That way, if IBM falls below $95, he will have a profit on the puts that will help ease the pain of the lower price on the stock. Meanwhile he can still collect the dividend.

Call options can also be used to protect a profit without actually having to take it. Suppose IBM rises to $110 from $100, but the investor doesn't want to sell yet. He can write calls on that stock, exercisable at $110 for a premium of, say, $5 each. If the stock stays at $110 or rises and the calls are exercised, he has a maximum profit before any dividends of $15 a share ($10 of price appreciation and the $5 collected for the option premium). However, if IBM falls to $105, he has protected his original $10 profit ($5 of price appreciation plus the $5 call premium). Writing calls can cushion a portfolio against loss.

Writing put options also can help an investor buy stock at a price cheaper than it is trading in the market. Say he wants to buy IBM, but it's trading at $102, and he wants to pay less than that. He can write put options with a $100 exercise price for a premium of, say, $3 a share. If the stock falls below $100 a share, the puts will be exercised and he will be obligated to buy stock at $100 a share. But he will have gotten it for a net price of $97 (the $100 purchase price less the $3 premium he collected on the puts), $5 below where it traded when he first sold the puts. If the price doesn't decline and the puts are never exercised, he has made a $3 a share profit on the premium.

Index Futures

The big difference between stock options and options on a market index is that the index option seller settles for *cash* instead of *stock* at expiration. The buyer of the index option limits his potential loss to the premium paid. But the seller has theoretically unlimited exposure. Futures contracts differ in that both buyers and sellers are obligated to perform. One must take delivery, and the other must deliver.

The options and futures markets became widely popular in the last 10 or 15 years, but they have been around for a long time. The Chicago Board of Trade is about 150 years old. Its offspring, the Chicago Board Options Exchange (CBOE), was founded in 1973. As the financial markets expanded in recent years, managers of large funds looked for ways to hedge their portfolios without having to buy individual options on each stock they held. In 1977, the Kansas City Board of Trade proposed that it be allowed to trade a futures contract tied to the Dow Jones Industrial Average.

Dow Jones decided against allowing the use of its index in this manner. In 1982, a futures contract based on the Value Line Composite Index began to trade in Kansas City.

Soon after, the Chicago Mercantile Exchange introduced a futures contract based on the Standard & Poor's index of 500 stocks. That was followed by the opening of the New York Futures Exchange, and trading in a contract based on the Big Board Composite Index.

The Commodities Futures Trading Commission, the agency that regulates the futures markets, then began a pilot program to permit trading in options on index futures contracts. An investor could buy a put or call on a futures contract subject to the same limitations and safeguards as any other option. At expiration, the investor could buy or sell the futures contract itself, rather than a specific stock or commodity.

The pilot program was judged a success, and index options began to sprout throughout the markets. In 1983, the Chicago Board Options Exchange introduced the first cash-settled option on its own CBOE 100 index. The American exchange soon followed with its own options contract tied to its Major Market Index. The CBOE later introduced options on the Standard & Poor's 500 Index and changed the name of the CBOE 100 to the S&P 100. The New York Stock Exchange began trading options on its own index, the Chicago Board of Trade offered futures trading on the American's Major Market Index, and the Philadelphia Stock

Exchange opened trading in options tied to the Value Line Index. Other options have been tested on indexes tied to over-the-counter stocks and on various subindexes on specific industry groups of stocks. Most of these fell flat and were delisted for lack of interest. But those tied to major market indexes have flourished, in large part because these options can be matched up against portfolios that are basically made up of an equivalent group of stocks (and because options are easily and quickly traded). The most popular of the index options is the S&P 100, traded on the Chicago Board of Trade. The S&P 500 futures contract, traded on the Chicago Board Options Exchange, is the most successful among index futures.

The popularity of these index futures and options is such that the total value of all contracts traded each day is greater than the total value of all shares of all companies listed on the New York Stock Exchange.

Chapter Four

STRATEGIES AND EXECUTION OF PROGRAM TRADING

The First Program

The trend towards indexing created the need for program trades. The first program trade was executed sometime in the middle 1970s, when index fund managers came on the scene seeking ways to effectively implement their strategy of replicating the S&P 500. Salo-

* The authors wish to thank Jeffrey S. Tabak, who served on President Reagan's Task Force on Market Mechanisms (the Brady Commission), for his contributions to the insights and material provided in this chapter.

mon Brothers is generally recognized as being the first broker to handle such a trade.

Brokerage firms already were capable of executing large transactions (often as much as hundreds of thousands of shares) because of their experience in block trading. Since the 1960s money managers had sought to buy and sell large numbers of shares in an individual stock quickly. Prior to block trading, that manager would have expected the broker to work the order over a long period of time. But in the 1960s, large brokerage firms recognized the need for immediacy and put up their own capital to facilitate transactions.

This was a period of growing institutionalization of the stock market; the number of large trades (larger than 10,000 shares) that took place on the New York Stock Exchange in 1965 constituted 3 percent of the average daily volume. In 1986, they had reached 50 percent.[1]

The giant brokerage firms, seeking to attract this business, began to commit their own capital to the other side of the transactions to execute the fund managers' orders. If, for example, a fund manager wanted to buy 10,000 shares, the broker would sell 10,000 shares to the managers at a negotiated price, and assume the risk of later having to buy those shares in order to cover the short sale. The trader thus acted as

---

[1] "New York Stock Exchange Fact Book."

both a broker and a dealer, buying and selling from his own inventory.

The willingness of large brokerage firms to assume the other side of their customers' transactions was an important actor on the stage being set for the first program trade. Some of these block transactions executed by large brokerage houses involved hundreds of thousands of shares and many millions of dollars, all being invested in one stock. The risk to the broker was not only the risk of the entire stock market rising or falling but also the specific-issue risk, that is, the risk that the specific company might, for example, make a surprise announcement. This dual role raised an interesting question: If the same person is now acting not only as broker—who traditionally represented a client, and introduced the buyer to the seller—but also as a dealer, himself making a market in the stock, was this not an apparent conflict of interest? Not really. If the broker's primary interest is to serve the customer, the willingness of large brokerage firms to act as intermediaries gave customers exactly what they needed to facilitate their orders in the marketplace.

By simultaneously trading a number of stocks, such as an index, the broker no longer runs the risk of the specific-issue fluctuation. The "issue" now is the market itself and the risk is spread throughout. This trading, program trading, evolved after one broker responded to the new needs of the money managers who had begun to think in terms of indexes and no longer in terms of specific issues.

> "It was around 1973, or 1974," recalls Salomon Brothers managing director Louis Margolis: "when index funds began to call us up and read us a list of stocks—200, 500, 1,000 of them—so we let them log on to our computer, and it would print away. And when it didn't come out fast enough, Stanley Shopkorn [Salomon's block-desk boss] would start yelling: 'Where's the damn program? We've got a program today!' "[2]

Salomon Brothers had the idea of guaranteeing their clients—the fund managers—precise execution, guaranteeing that they would be in the index at the closing price of the day before the starting date. All funds' performances traditionally are measured from a starting date . . . Day One, if you will. Index fund managers are measured from that given date as to how well or poorly they replicated the S&P 500. Salomon promised the managers they would start out Day One having bought the index "in one fell swoop" at the closing price of the day before. The "one fell swoop" constituted the "program." That guarantee had large ramifications, both for the broker (in this case Salomon Brothers) and for the overall stock market.

Suppose a broker had to buy 5,500 shares of IBM as part of replicating the index as of Friday's closing price. The fund manager is guaranteed he'll own 5,500 shares of IBM at whatever that price turns out to be. Theoretically, then, at some point on Friday, the bro-

---

[2] Excerpted in Lenny Glynn and Saul Hansell, "Packaged Goods," *Institutional Investor*, September 1988, p. 5.

ker is in the market trying to amass 5,500 shares. He wants to make sure he buys the stock at an average price that is either equal to or lower than the closing price. If the closing price turns out to be lower than what he bought at and he has guaranteed the client the closing price, then the broker absorbs the loss.

One might also find a situation in which the broker does not, or is not able to, buy the stock on that day and thus is short the stock. The broker must try to buy it on a later occasion. If he ultimately pays a higher price at the later date than what he guaranteed the client, the broker must absorb *that* loss.

Notwithstanding the possible risks, this kind of business was perceived by brokerage firms as very attractive because (1) they were able to charge commissions; and (2) the risk that they'd have a gain or loss on the customer's order was less than the risk involved in block trading of one stock.

Initially, brokers competed for this kind of business by being willing to charge smaller commissions. As of May 1, 1975, all commission rates were deemed negotiable. Theoretically, a broker involved in program trading could charge no commission. Brokers like to have significant order flow to show other potential customers. The order-flow feature was so attractive that, at times, a firm would be willing to guarantee that the customer received the closing price, even if the broker had not had the opportunity to act in the market during that day but had to wait until the following day to execute the order. That subjected the broker to overnight risk, while also guaranteeing the money manager that his closing price had not been driven up by his own broker's activity. For that added risk, some brokers sought higher commissions. Still, the transactions remained appealing to both sides, and program trading continued. For the next several years, however, its application would remain one of investment or divestment of monies in index funds.

Index Arbitrage

In 1982, the first derivative product that was based on an index came into existence. It was a future on an index of 1500 stocks published by Value Line that traded on the Kansas City Futures Exchange. Later that year, the Chicago Mercantile Exchange created a future that was based on the S&P 500 Index. The creation of index options and futures led to the development of index arbitrage, an activity which, by the mid-80s, had generated the need for program trades. Index arbitrage would catapult program trading onto the front pages of the financial press.

Index arbitrage takes advantage of disparities between the prices of the same stock in two different markets, playing off the price differences between the index derivatives (futures or options) and the basket of stocks that make up the index. The firm of Miller Tabak Hirsch + Co. (MTH, this author's company) was one of the first to organize itself to do index arbitrage, having initiated the strategy in 1982 with the Kansas City future.

When that first future traded on Kansas City, traditional cash and carry calculation (that is, the time value of money) showed the future to be selling significantly below its fair value. Therefore, the simple exercise of buying the future, selling short stocks comprising the Index (in this case the Value Line Index), earning interest on the short sale proceeds minus the dividends payable, and earning a trading profit on the discounted future would lock in a sizable profit at no risk.

By the end of 1982, the futures contract based on the S&P 500 (the index most widely used by professional money managers) established itself as the most heavily traded futures contract. Then, early in 1983, the Chicago Board of Options introduced an option on an index, the S&P 100 (known as the OEX). Like the future, the option did not result in the delivery of stock but rather settled in cash. Also in 1983, the American Stock Exchange introduced its first index option, the Major Market Index (known as the MMI). These quickly became the most popular index options.

Miller Tabak Hirsch's idea was simple: create a long position (that is, one that would gain if the index rose) by establishing certain option positions, and create a short position (that is, one that would lose if the index rose) by selling all the stocks in the index on which the option was based.

What does it mean to buy or sell "all the stocks in the index"? How does one calculate how many shares of each stock to buy? Let's pretend for a moment that we have an index comprised of the three largest companies: International Business Machines (IBM), Exxon (XON), and General Electric (GE). Our index is to be capitalization weighted; that is, the contribution of each company to the index will be weighted according to the market value of the stock (which is computed by multiplying the shares outstanding of each company times its respective stock price).

TABLE FOUR

	Shares Outstanding	Stock Price	Market Value
IBM	593,138,000	122⅞	$72,881,832,000
XON	1,379,000,000	44¾	61,710,250,000
GE	902,953,000	43⅝	39,391,325,000
		TOTAL	$173,983,407,000

We see the market value of the three companies exceeds $173 billion. But it would be absurd to report that, in today's trading, this particular index rose from $173,983,407,000 to $176,858,498,000, which is what would happen if each stock rose one point. To make the situation more manageable, a divisor is used. A divisor is a number we have chosen to divide into the market value. The devisor we will choose is the number

695,933,000, chosen because it will generate an "easy-to-say" number.

TABLE FIVE

	Day 1	Day 2
Total Market Value	$173,983,407,000	$176,858,498,000
Divisor	÷ 695,933,000	÷ 695,933,000
3-Stock Index	= 250.00	= 254.13

Once we use the divisor, the value of our three-stock index will be stated at 250.00 on Day 1 or, after a point rise on each stock, at 254.13 on Day 2. This manufactured representation of value now resembles the value we see for a well-known index like the S + P 500 (which, at the time of this writing, stands at 264.12).

The next step is to create an index option or future based on our three-stock index. Arbitrarily, we decide that we want the option or future to be based on stock worth: on Day 1, $25,000 and on Day 2, $25,413. Notice that the decimal in the index has been moved two spots to the right and a dollar sign was added (250.00 to $25,000 and 254.13 to $25,413). The same result is achieved by changing the divisor from 695,933,000 to 6,959,330.

TABLE SIX

	DAY 1	DAY 2
Total Market Value	$173,983,407,000	$176,858,498,000
Divisor	÷ 6,959,330	÷ 6,959,330
3-Stock value for option or future	$25,000	$25,413

To determine how many shares of each stock go into the value for our options or futures, we take the divisor and divide it into the shares outstanding of each stock.

TABLE SEVEN

SHARES OUTSTANDING

IBM	593,138,000	÷ 6,959,330	= 85.23	shs
XON	1,379,000,000	÷ 6,959,330	= 198.15	shs
GE	902,953,000	÷ 6,959,330	= 129.75	shs

TABLE EIGHT

	DAY 1		DAY 2	
IBM 85.23 shs X $122^7/_8$ =	$10,472.64	$123^7/_8$ =	$10,557.87
XON 198.15 shs X $44^3/_4$ =	8,867.21	$45^3/_4$ =	9,065.36
GE 129.75 shs X $43^5/_8$ =	5,660.34	$44^5/_8$ =	5,790.09
	$25,000.19		$ 25,413.32

Thus we see exactly how many shares we would have to buy to exactly match the index. In the real world, of course, we ignore partial shares.

If one buys the long position at a cheaper price than one sells the short position, a profit is automatically achieved. From the summer of 1983 onward, this is precisely what Miller Tabak Hirsch actively did—they went long on the Index options and went short on the stock. Soon thereafter, a future on the Major Market Index (MMI) began trading on The Chicago Board of Trade, and Miller Tabak Hirsch + Co. began index arbitraging between the futures and the index. On page 106 is the "real-life" example of that strategy in operation.

For months, Miller Tabak Hirsch + Co. had the field to themselves. Most brokers couldn't imagine trying to trade 100 stocks simultaneously and coordinating that effort with trading in the index options. Actually, the logistics were not too difficult to implement. The firm organized a group of floor brokers on the NYSE to handle the executions of the stocks in the different areas of the exchange, and also used the Designated Order Turnaround System (DOT), the Exchange's electronic execution system, for the smaller stocks, bypassing the floor brokers and going directly to the specialist themselves. As most NYSE floor brokers had never before been involved in a program, it was extremely important to find brokers with the right frame of mind to be able to quickly delegate a group of stocks to the proper posts, the locations on the exchange floor where stocks trade.

A REAL-LIFE STRATEGY FOR MAKING 14% RISK-FREE

■ On Feb. 26, Jeffrey Miller of the New York brokerage firm Miller Tabak Hirsch & Co. bought 2,000 shares each of the 20 stocks that make up the Major Market Index (MMI). He paid $2,749,000, putting down half in cash and borrowing the rest at 8.5%.

■ Simultaneously, he sold short 35 futures contracts on the MMI expiring on Mar. 21. Each futures contract was priced at 313.55, while the MMI itself stood at 311.74. The idea was to profit from the spread—in this case, 1.81—between the futures and the index. The value of each futures contract is the price multiplied by $250. So Miller's books were credited for $78,387.50 per contract (313.55 x $250) for a total of $2,743,563.

The 20 stocks that make up the Major Market Index	Price paid on Feb. 26	Price at closing bell on Mar. 21	Dividends paid between dates
American Express	64	65⅝	
AT&T	22½	22⅞	
Chevron	37⅞	37⅜	
Coca-Cola	92	103⅜	$0.78
Dow Chemical	48¾	52⅜	
Du Pont	70½	72½	
Eastman Kodak	55	59¾	
Exxon	54⅞	54¾	
General Electric	75½	75¾	0.58
General Motors	78¼	83¼	
IBM	158⅛	148½	
International Paper	57	60	
Johnson & Johnson	48⅜	54	
Merck	150¾	161¼	0.90
3M	97¼	104	
Mobil Oil	30⅛	29½	
Philip Morris	101⅛	119¼	1.15
Procter & Gamble	67	73½	
Sears	42⅞	46⅛	
U. S. Steel	22⅝	22¾	
MAJOR MARKET INDEX	**311.74**	**328.07**	
FUTURES ON MMI	**313.55**	**328.07**	

■ Miller had no idea which way the market would move, but he knew he couldn't lose. That's because at 4 p.m. on Mar. 21, the futures on the MMI and the index itself would have to be equal. Miller didn't care if the stocks fell, because the futures, which were priced above the index, would fall farther. So the loss on his stocks would be more than offset by the profit from the short sale of the futures.

■ As things worked out, the opposite happened. Stocks moved up sharply, and so did the futures—but not as much, because the spread disappears at expiration. In this case, his profit from the stocks exceeded his loss from the short sale of the futures.

■ As the market closed on Mar. 21, Miller sold all his stocks and allowed his futures contracts to expire. Here's how Miller fared:

INCOME		
PROFIT ON STOCKS		
Amount received on Mar. 21	$2,893,000	
Amount paid on Feb. 26	2,749,000	$144,000
DIVIDENDS		6,820
COSTS		
INTEREST on $1,374,500		−8,438
LOSS ON FUTURES		
Amount credited on Feb. 26	2,743,563	
Amount debited on expiration	2,870,613	−127,050
MILLER'S TRANSACTION FEES		−1,100
NET PROFIT		**$14,232**
ORIGINAL INVESTMENT		**$1,374,500**
ANNUALIZED RETURN ON INVESTMENT		**14.34%**
TREASURY BILL RATE		**6.80**
BONUS RISK-FREE RETURN		**7.54**

SOURCE: Business Week, April 7, 1986, p. 34.

Figure Six.

Many firms also have had difficulty with the concept of how the trades will be unwound, and how positions will be closed out on expiration day. Even if they were successful in putting the positions on initially, how could they ever be successfully unwound? Miller Tabak Hirsch was one of the first firms to use the "market-on-close" concept. This is a rule that has been in existence for a long time but was rarely used and had never been connected with arbitrage. Quite simply, positions are closed out on expiration day by buying all the stocks on the closing bell at 4 PM. The total value of all the stocks would, by definition, equal the value of the future. Since the future settles for cash, the future and the stocks will, in essence, converge at the 4 PM bell.

For months, Miller Tabak Hirsch was able to quickly and successfully execute market-on-close orders at 4:00 PM on expiration Fridays. However, due to the Good Friday holiday, expiration in April 1984 fell on a Thursday. The impact of the market-on-close concept would change dramatically that day. Trading had been light all morning and many traders left early for a long weekend. Shortly before the bell, several floor traders in the OEX pit in Chicago sold the near-term calls short, assuming they would expire worthless. Within an hour before the bell, Miller Tabak Hirsch had sent market-on-close orders to all the specialists with a total aggregate value approaching $100 million. Although small by today's standards, that batch of orders was probably the largest market-on-close program ever to that date. The specialists, on the eve of a long weekend, found only a small sell interest for this buy-on-the-close program.

Therefore, when the blocks "printed" (or traded; reports are seen on the tape) on big "upticks" (when the next trade is at a higher trade than the previous trade) at 4:00, everyone was stunned to see what was occurring. The "worthless" calls that the floor traders in Chicago had just sold short suddenly had real value and they were scrambling to cover their positions. Everyone was endeavoring to understand why all this block activity suddenly occurred from a brokerage firm almost no one had heard of.

Soon, the enormous growth in the impact of expiration Friday resulted in the days themselves becoming labelled "Triple Witching Hours." Traders now understood the ease with which positions could be unwound without any risk. The fear that one illiquid stock in an index could hurt the arbitrage opportunities was alleviated because no matter what price that illiquid stock printed on the bell (transacted at the close of business, which is signalled by the ringing of a bell), that price would be reflected in the corresponding option or future. Stock, stock options, and futures would always converge at 4:00 at the expiration. This convergence concept, made so crystal clear to everyone by Miller Tabak's buy program on April 19, 1984, magnified the growth of derivative products in geometric proportions.

While the profit potential from this kind of index arbitrage is alluring, substantial risks are involved.

The relationships between the options and futures in Chicago and the stocks in New York exist only for very short periods of time. Because of these inherent risks, these trades cannot possibly be done by an individual investor. The individual investor could not act promptly enough through his retail broker to take advantage of those price discrepancies. Moreover, commissions costs, which an NYSE member firm like Miller Tabak Hirsch + Co. does not have, would absorb a tremendous amount of the potential profit.

The largest risk to the professional trader is the execution risk. Execution risks covers a broad spectrum of occurrences. First, now that many more brokerage firms are involved in index arbitrage, the number of times during the day in which price discrepancies exist have become far fewer. Therefore, the trader may only have split seconds to act before more normalized pricing is re-established between the markets. Second, given the increasing volatility of the marketplace, the trader may experience a great deal of difficulty in shorting stocks: a potential profit may become a whopping loss. Remember that a short sale can only be executed on a uptick—the price of the stock cannot be below the previous last sale.

The problem in "getting shorts off" arises from several sources. For example, suppose a significant, negative international news event hits the Dow Jones tape while one is trying to sell stocks short. The trader will be unable to execute those shorts as an avalanche of selling hits the market. Thus the trader is left holding long futures or options which are declining in value without any corresponding offset in short stock.

Another problem in getting short orders filled is that other index arbitrageurs will be attempting to do the same thing in exactly the same stocks. Thus, the trader must be extremely sensitive to the size of the index arbitrage program he is trying to complete. This sensitivity can only come from the experience of dealing with a myriad of stocks and developing a sense in each security as to the number of shares that can be easily shorted on a plus tick. One can then balance the size of the index arbitrage attempted at various times during the trading day. An intimate knowledge of the size of trades in individual equities, as well as the options and the futures, is essential to the successful completion of an index arbitrage situation.

A third facet of execution risk relates to the specifics of the futures. Unlike the NYSE, there is no real tape for futures showing each transaction in order of execution; nor are the price, parity, and priority rules as clearly established. Under the "open outcry" system, the trader must be sure he is represented by a talented broker in the crowd who is able to get his orders completed. Otherwise, the trader can find himself short stocks without owning any futures, or have the futures orders completed at prices that make the arbitrage considerably less profitable.

Another type of risk involved in these trades is one of "early exercise." Assume the trader has a position of long call, short put, and short stock, which is a perfectly hedged arbitrage. However, if the market were to decline dramatically, the put might rise in value to the point where it is trading at parity to its index value. An investor who is long that put (that is, you own the put) might choose to exercise his put if he feels the market has declined enough and he wants to take a profit on the put.

Unfortunately for the index arbitrageur, his position is now long call and short stock without any short put position. He is no longer perfectly hedged: if the market were to rise dramatically the next day, his loss on the short stock would most likely not be offset by the rise in the value of the call. His winning position would become a loser.

Because of this early exercise risk, money arbitrageurs prefer the SPX options (options on the S&P 500 Index) over the OEX options (options on the S&P 100 Index) on the Chicago Board Options Exchange, because the SPX options are "European style": by definition, they cannot be exercised early. It is interesting to note that, effective with the January 1989 series, the American Stock Exchange switched the Major Market Index (MMI) options to European style.

Another type of risk relates to interest rate volatility. Assume that the cost of borrowing the stocks is 8.5%. If interest rates rise dramatically while the position is on, obviously the profit potential will diminish as it will cost more to carry the position. Similarly, a drop in interest rates will increase the rate of return. Because of the interest rate risk, most arbitrageurs tend to execute trades with less than 90 days until expiration.

When the general public hears the terms index arbitrage or program trading, the perception is one of massive computers executing huge transactions with price insensitivity. The reality differs greatly from this perception. In fact, a good trader uses the computer merely as a tool to alert him to profit-generating situations. While a computer can be programmed to indicate to the trader that an arbitrage situation exists, the computer itself does not do the trading.

The computer helps ensure that sides of the arbitrage will be entered on the respective trading floors in New York and Chicago within seconds. When an arbitrageur attempts to execute both the options and the stocks at the same time, the computer is incapable of indicating which side of the trade to execute first. This is because this determination is not simply a mechanical process, but is a "thinking" function. It is up to the trader to make the important decisions: should all the futures be bought at once immediately after entering the short stock orders, or should only a few futures be purchased until it is clear that the short sales will be executed? What should the trader do if the market explodes to the upside before all the futures are purchased? The computer cannot answer these questions.

The trader's perception of the near-term direction of the market is vitally important in optimizing the potential profit. While computers are extremely useful in spotting an arbitrage situation, computers do not have "perception." That is why index arbitrage is done by individuals and not by computers, and why individuals produce different rates of return on what appear to be the same trades.

This entire investment concept has been extremely controversial: many blame index arbitrage for causing huge swings in the market averages. We believe, instead, that index arbitrage brings a significant amount of liquidity to the marketplace. When huge sell orders flood the market in either stocks or futures, the index arbitrageur can often serve as a buffer by buying either the basket of stocks or the future when one or the other gets "cheap" and an arbitrage opportunity evolves.

The index arbitrageur is not attempting to knock the market down violently or raise it artificially. His only task is to eliminate price discrepancies that exist between the different products and return those prices to their "fair" value.

Moreover, one can argue that index arbitrage allows more traditional money managers to execute their trades with greater rapidity and efficiency. If a money manager wishes to sell several blocks of stocks, he can often find a buyer for those securities during an index arbitrage program where stocks are being bought and futures sold. Without index arbitrage, that money manager might be selling those securities at a much lower price. Index arbitrage, therefore, can be viewed as aiding overall portfolio management capabilities.

Furthermore, traditional portfolio managers are now getting more "efficient" prices on the sale of their individual securities. If a fund manager is in the marketplace selling a group of stocks he no longer likes, the index arbitrageur will be bidding for those stocks at prices that reflect "fair market value" relative to the futures. While program-trader bashing makes for provocative cocktail-party chatter, the reality of the situation is far different from the perception.

There is one form of program trading, however, which is detrimental to efficiency and liquidity: portfolio insurance. Portfolio insurance is very different from index arbitrage; it is a concept in which a computer indicates the number of futures contracts to be sold to protect an equity portfolio in case of a huge price drop. The problem with this concept is that it does not account for the possibility that futures prices will drop dramatically when everybody using this strategy attempts to sell futures at the same time. Unlike index arbitrage, portfolio insurance is not price-sensitive with regard to the actual level at which the future is executed. This can cause extreme disruptions to the marketplace, resulting in illiquidity and panic. This is what occurred on October 19, 1987. As the Brady Commission stated, "This initial (price) decline ignited mechanical, price-insensitive selling by a number of institutions employing portfolio insurance strategies."[3]

---

[3] "The Role of Index-Related Trading in the Market Decline on September 11 and 12, 1986," A Report by the U.S. Securities and Exchange Commission, Division of Market Regulation, March 1987, Executive Summary.

114

Portfolio insurance is a flawed concept and its flaws were dramatically revealed on Black Monday. Practitioners of this theory have become so disillusioned that it is estimated that less than 50 percent of stock once covered by portfolio insurance before the crash is still "insured." While portfolio insurance is essentially dead, index arbitrage is thriving because of its ability to link the markets efficiently.

Why didn't index arbitrage provide liquidity and efficiency on October 19? Because the price discovery mechanism failed to exist. Due to the enormous shares covered by portfolio insurance, the index arbitrageur had no way of knowing what the actual prices of either stocks or futures or options were and so could not effectively link the markets. Because futures prices were falling so rapidly under the weight of portfolio insurance, and stock prices were also falling, index arbitrageurs effectively removed themselves from the marketplace and stood on the sidelines. Index arbitrage depends on precision pricing and quick executions and reports. Aside from the speed of the price changes, quick reports were virtually impossible due to the crushing volume, inability of clerks and brokers to handle that volume, and the virtual breakdown of the DOT system.

The growth of index arbitrage points to another important concept: the inexorable link between stocks, stock index futures, and options. These vehicles really constitute one market. While they should not necessarily be regulated by one body, any changes in one product directly affect the others. An index arbitrage is really one portfolio rather than three distinct products in different marketplaces. Thus, in dealing with such controversial issues as margin requirements, the "one-market concept" must be grappled with to assure that changes in a particular product do not have dire liquidity consequences for the overall market.

While the capital markets will always have a limited ability to deal with the kind of one-sided volume witnessed on October 19, markets and products that enhance liquidity are what need to be strengthened. In the asset allocation-driven world in which we now exist, the importance of the derivative products in enhancing the ability to redirect large pools of assets quickly can't be stressed too heavily. Liquidity is what moves merchandise and index arbitrage has clearly demonstrated its capacity to strengthen the liquidity factor, although not without a good deal of controversy.

Index arbitrage since October 19 has remained extremely controversial, despite the fact that not one of the post-crash studies found it culpable of that day's disaster. As liquidity has been strained in all markets, it appears that some of the true arbitrage linkage has been tainted. Instead of merely remaining on the sidelines until the arbitrage opportunity appears, many firms are forcing the trade by "legging" one side and not executing the other side of the trade for several minutes or even hours. "Legging" means that only one side of the arbitrage is executed, as the trader is betting that the market will move in a particular direction. This is a more aggressive tactic which is beyond the bounds of classic index arbitrage and serves to heighten volatility. For example, if a trader is bullish, he might buy the futures in the morning and not sell the stocks until late that afternoon. If he is right, the financial rewards can be much larger. However, under this scenario, the linkage factor between the markets is misrepresented and this type of trading can be disruptive to the marketplace. Indeed, legging activity appears to have been responsible for some of the extreme volatility witnessed on days like January 8, 1988, when the Dow plummeted 140 points. Several commentators also have suggested that brokerage firms sold futures below fair market value in proprietary accounts in order to create a cascading market effect, then covered short positions later in the day at tremendous profits. While such behavior is difficult to prove conclusively, one would hope that firms would not sacrifice the productivity and efficiency the index arbitrage provides by corrupting that function for short-term-trading profits.

Other Program Trades

Program trading is used by portfolio managers to accomplish a number of purposes in addition to index arbitrage.

The decision to create an indexed portfolio, for example, might require the removal of a previously held portfolio: Get rid of Group A; buy Group B. Both actions are instances of program trading. Or a fund manager may wish to change the basic asset mix within a portfolio, in anticipation of some event occurring in the market. Such an event might be the superior performance of one sector such as utilities, or the under performance of another such as large capitalization companies. Each side of that bet could require a program trade.

In the days following the crash of October 1987, Miller Tabak Hirsch + Co. received an order from a money manager to sell off $50 million worth of telephone utility stocks from a larger list of those stocks and to substitute with $50 million of diversified large capitalization companies. The money manager put the order not in terms of selling X number of shares of X Telephone Company, but rather choosing from the portfolio any $50 million worth of telephone shares that quickly could be sold. During the crash, this money manager had held a larger weighting of utility stocks in his portfolio than was representative of the market as a whole. Though the crash affected those stocks, the decline was less than for other sectors. The money manager thus had achieved a superior relative performance, and wanted to lock in that performance by reducing the weighting in utilities and increasing the weightings in other stocks back to their normal levels.

In executing this trade, Miller Tabak Hirsch used two techniques. First, they created a list of several of the utility stocks held by the money manager whose total value would equal approximately $1 million, as well as a second list made up of shares of the large capital stocks whose value also would equal $1 million. Then each of those lists was programmed into the DOT system so that at propitious moments during the day, as the market rose and fell, a one-button press would automatically sell the $1 million utilities list or buy the $1 million large capital list. This was done a number of times throughout the day.

The second technique involved constantly sifting through the telephone stocks by the money manager and selling those that were up the most in the day's (or prior day's) trading and buying from the diversified list of large cap stocks those which had fallen during those days' trading. This was *not* the traditional buying and selling of under- or overvalued stocks. This was taking advantage of short-term fluctuations that were nothing more than noise in the marketplace. The names of the companies whose stocks were bought and sold were irrelevant. The program was everything.

Actually, one can see that there were several programs involved. The money manager phrased *his* initial request in terms of aggregates, Miller Tabak Hirsch did both sides of the execution in terms of aggregates, and DOT transacted it all in aggregate amounts.

Execution Costs

Execution costs are always a major concern to managers of large assets. Program trading is a method for reducing and controlling execution costs.

In the lexicon of Wall Street, a trade like the one cited above is known as *agency packaging*. The portfolio manager forms the list of stocks into one composite asset and asks a broker as agent to handle the transaction. The broker is given the list in the program ahead of time. This is also called an *open-hand* transaction. The broker grants a volume discount on commission— a few cents a share—that is below the normal commission for stock-by-stock trading. The broker assumes no risk and acts purely as the fund manager's agent in trading a composite asset as if it were a single stock.

The costs of executing a stock order begin with the broker's commission, which for large orders from institutional clients can amount to five cents or less per share. Much more significant costs are the bid-ask spread cost and impact costs. Even stocks that trade on the New York Stock Exchange are subject to a bid-ask spread. For a stock whose last sale was at 50, this means the current market might consist of buyers willing to pay $50 (the bid) and sellers willing to sell at $50.25 (the offer). Although investment analysis may tell us that a stock is an attractive purchase at $50 per share, under these circumstances, the effort to buy the stock at $50 might force the price above $50. We would be deceiving ourselves if we thought we could buy the stock at $50, when the cheapest price available is $50.25. By the same token, the stock we sold in order to finance the purchase of the new stock also might have incurred the same type of cost from the bid-ask spread. Paying 25 cents a share twice creates a cost of one percent—that is, it reduces performance by one percent compared to making no changes in the portfolio.

In addition, there is no guarantee that we can buy all the stock we want even at $50.25, for our actions as buyers has impact on what our costs will be. We might have to reach to $50.50 or even to $51. The outcome will depend on what price level sellers will emerge at and how much competition there will be from other buyers who wish to purchase the stock.

This situation led to the development of the *guaranteed package* form of transaction. The idea behind the guaranteed package was to eliminate the uncertainty about transaction costs that confronts the portfolio manager seeking to make significant portfolio adjustment. In a guaranteed package, the broker guarantees that the client will receive specified prices on each stock in the package of stocks. The aggregate price for all these stocks is called the strike price. The broker and money manager also agree as to exactly when the transaction will take place.

Typically, the strike price will be the closing price on the NYSE. But it might instead be either the closing price from a trading session already completed or the closing price from a session yet to take place. In the first instance, a broker guarantees that the client receive last night's closing price plus or minus some specific amount, depending on whether the client is buying or selling. The broker reviews the list of stocks sent by the money manager and decides on the basis of liquidity and volatility how large the plus or minus will be. Competing brokers then submit their bids to the money manager with varying sizes of premiums offered or discounts asked for.

One well-publicized account of a *guaranteed package* involved the State of New Jersey's various retirement systems' decision to rearrange their portfolios to exclude the stocks of companies doing business in South Africa. State officials called on several major Wall Street brokerage firms inviting them to bid one price for the stocks to be sold. The firms were shown the list of stocks to be sold before the opening of trading on a given day. The strike price was to be last night's closing price minus a broker's discount. The winning broker would be the one who quoted the smallest discount. Once the day's trading began the broker would be in a rush to sell the shares at prices not far off last night's close (or, at worst, at differences small enough to be covered by the discount). The discount might range from a few pennies a share to twenty-five cents a share or even higher.

From the point of view of the money manager, this transaction accomplished one important goal: It pinned down the cost of the trade. Even a certain cost of twenty-five cents might be preferable to an unknown cost.

Guaranteed packages are capable of affecting the entire market even though only designated stocks are involved in the transaction. From the opening bell the broker is, in a sense, the owner of the shares and is at risk to the movement of the entire market. The broker might seek to eliminate this market risk by selling S&P 500 Index futures. That sale would cause downward pressure of the S&P future's price which then would lead to a situation ripe for index arbitrage. The index arbitrage player taking the other side of the broker's sales would buy the now-discounted future while simultaneously selling the stocks in the index, thus pushing down the market.

The benefit of the guaranteed trade-fixed costs is apparent, but so is the problem: How can the private investor have confidence in the stock market when his most recent purchase might quickly be sent into a fall by the playing out of a large sell program? In the long run, the value of all stocks is enhanced by the capacity of the market mechanism to move large amounts of stock quickly and cheaply. A single investor might lose on a specific trade through bad luck in timing, but if we consider taking all the investors in the aggregate, the value of that "mass" portfolio will be strengthened.

The New Jersey South African trade was completed on an open-hand basis: all the stocks were identified to the competing brokers. However, if a money manager were to use as the strike price the closing prices of a session yet to be completed, he or she might not be so anxious to have the broker know the names of the stocks in advance. The broker might then be able to pattern his trades so as to arrive at the highest closing price. For example, were this broker to give a client a report that the client bought X number of shares, at that day's closing price, the broker might be tempted to jump the gun, make early purchases, and thus drive up the final price. To counter this temptation, money mangers seeking to do program trades developed so-called closed-hand strategies, which involve blind bids. In the *blind bid* approach, the broker guarantees a strike price for the portfolio, but does so sight unseen. The fund manager does not reveal the specific stocks in the program, nor the size of the blocks, though he will reveal enough characteristics about the parcel so that the broker can bid a price and a commission level. For instance, the broker might be told that the stocks are all from the S&P 500 and that no block is larger than a normal day's trading, or that the mix is a certain percentage of stocks on the NYSE, the American Stock Exchange, and NASDAQ. He might learn, too, that the program is an index subset.

The more the broker knows, the closer he can tailor his bid. Further, if he knows or summarizes that the program reflects an index, he can hedge his now considerable risk with index futures and options. But additional risk now assumed by the broker may result in additional cost to the money manager in the form of increased premiums or smaller discounts. Still, if it assures that the program will be executed at an efficient market price, the net cost is justified. Blind bids also can be let to several brokers, who bid competitively, thus holding down costs.

An extreme closed-hand transaction is the *double-blind* bid. Nobody is told anything. The broker guarantees a price, but he doesn't know the exact composition of the program nor the time when the list will be delivered to him so that he may start trading it, though it is usually delivered at the market's close. Because his risk is much greater—world war could break out between the time of his bid and the time of the trade—so is his commission.

A variation on this scheme might be called the *multiple open hand blind-date bid*, described by one money manager thusly: "To make the program trade, we would get the brokers to set up three different portfolios, each with a hundred names." The brokers would prepare these lists of stocks (the "names" as supplied by the manager) in their own computers in such a manner that at a signal they transmit these names to the stock exchange as orders via the DOT or other order transmittal system for simultaneous execution. But the brokers would not execute the program trade until told to do so by the manager.

> We would tell the brokers that in the next couple of days we would probably go with one of these portfolios, then the next day we flip a coin: Heads we trade; tails, no trade today. The next day we flip the coin again and decide to trade portfolio A, B, or C. In the late afternoon, we tell the broker that we will trade portfolio C on the opening tomorrow at the price of the close half an hour ago.[4]

This particular transaction is a hybrid, since the brokers know the names in the portfolios that will be traded, but they don't know which portfolio will be traded or when. The manager has chosen this particular strategy for a couple of reasons. By letting the broker know what stocks he wants to trade, even though he doesn't tell the broker precisely which, the broker can estimate his risk more closely and thus calculate

---

[4] Jeremy Grantham, Grantham Mayo Van Otterloo.

his price more finely. By not telling the broker on which day he will trade and precisely which stocks he will trade, the manager also assures himself that no one will leap into the market ahead of him and perhaps upset the pricing on the stocks he wants to trade.

Another way of solving the conflicting interests of broker and client has been through the use of incentives. Instead of determining a fixed commission based on the guaranteed price and the broker's risk, the portfolio manager and the broker may negotiate an incentive package. Instead of a guaranteed price, they may agree on a benchmark price. The closer to the benchmark the broker manages to execute the program, the higher his fee. Or perhaps the broker and the client will split any savings the broker manages to effect beyond the benchmark.

Sometimes parts of a program may prove to be indigestible on the market, a reminder that program trades are in fact a lot of individual trades. This may happen when a portfolio contains many small-capitalization, thinly traded stocks. The broker may not be able to move them and the portfolio manager may then resort to incentive either with the same broker or with another broker, in which the broker makes his best effort to move the stocks at or near agreed-on prices. The broker will share in any improvement on the benchmark prices.

The program trading relationship between broker and money-manager client begins to resemble an exotic dance. But it is the underlying objective that matters, and that is how to best make a major change in a portfolio of assets. Perhaps the most significant change that can be made through portfolio rebalancing, and one that leads to a need for program trading, is a swap of stocks for bonds or bonds for stocks. In a bond program trade, a manager might sell the stock portfolio and replace it with the purchase of a carefully designed portfolio of bonds. The reason for the carefulness is that the manager might want to match the money flows from a bond portfolio with the actual payment of benefits. It is not uncommon for large swap programs to affect the market for several days, ultimately moving the Dow Jones Average by many points.

Once again, one can sympathize with the private investor who has had the misfortune of buying a stock just before a large retirement plan decides to dump stock in favor of bonds. In the days when such a move could take place only through the combined actions of many investors, one might find their own mistimed investment decision easier to swallow. But when a single pension officer at a single pension plan can effect the same outcome, then we can feel for the private investor caught in the current. However, our experience has been that most of those caught in such sudden tides are not serious long-term investors but rather trader-activists who are gambling as much as investing.

As we stated earlier, a market that can handle billion dollar trades efficiently and without serious long-term ruptures is a market that ultimately enhances the value of all investors' assets.

Portfolio Insurance

The program trades discussed previously were done as the result of decisions made about a portfolio—choosing one group of stocks over another, choosing bonds over stocks, and so on. A very different kind of strategy that also uses program trading is portfolio insurance.

In portfolio insurance, one does not make a decision about possible investment return; one acts based upon what had just occurred in the market. As we have indicated, the idea behind portfolio insurance is to limit the loss from market declines while also maintaining the opportunity to profit from market rises. The user of portfolio insurance is willing to accept some cost for that tradeoff.

Figure Seven illustrates the relationship between insurance cost and market returns. The unbroken line on the axis represents the correlation between the market line (the market's rise or fall) and the investor line (an investor's gain or loss) without portfolio insurance. The broken line represents that correlation when portfolio insurance is used. The difference between the broken and unbroken lines, both in the gains category (above the market line) and in the loss category (below the market line) is the cost of portfolio insurance.

In the example shown here, if the market were to rise by five percent, the profit of the investor *without* portfolio insurance also would rise by five percent. Were the

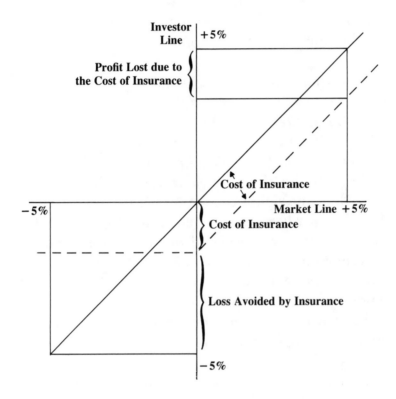

Figure Seven

market to fall by five percent, that investor's loss would also be five percent. The investor *with* insurance, on the other hand, would give up a portion of the rise when the market rose by five percent, but would avoid considerable loss when the market fell by five percent.

129

The pattern of the broken line being sought (one of truncated losses) can be achieved using two different methods of portfolio insurance, one a static strategy and the other a dynamic strategy. Both strategies can lead to program trades with significant consequences for the stock market as a whole.

Static portfolio insurance requires the purchase of a put option, which (as we explained in Chapter Three) gives the holder the right to sell stock at a predetermined price. For example, if the S&P 500 stood at 250, one could purchase for approximately $5.00 a put option with the life of approximately 90 days, that gave the holder the right to sell at 240. If the market were to drop below 240 anytime during the 90-day period, the holder of the option would incur no loss beyond the four percent decline from 250 to 240. On the other hand, if the market rose from 250 to 275 within that 90-day period, the option holder would show only an eight percent gain, once the cost of the option was taken into consideration.

This process generates a program trade: The person from whom the option was purchased originally hedges that put sale by selling S&P 500 futures. This act exerts subsequent downward pressure on the market, which then leads to the initiation of index arbitrage, which, as we have seen, brings about the sale of stock in the form of a program trade.

Dynamic portfolio insurance also generates program trades but with somewhat differing consequences. In this method, the risk of market decline is reduced by use of a program that will automatically sell stocks after a pre-set point of market decline has occurred. Should the market decline even further, more stocks will be sold automatically, with the ultimate outcome of a stock-free portfolio in the event of total market fall.

Another way of reducing one's stock exposure by using the dynamic form of insurance would be to sell stock futures while retaining the actual stocks. This act would also exert downward pressure on the futures market, which in turn would bring a new buyer into the market, one eager to buy up the discounted futures. That buyer, of course, would be hedging himself by selling *his* stocks as part of a program.

In the static form, then, the purchase of a put leads immediately to the sale of stock in the form of a program trade; whereas, in the dynamic form, the sale of stock either directly or indirectly (through the sale of futures leading to index arbitrage) only takes place after the market has moved. Though the goals of both forms are the same, the effect on the stock market is in one case immediate, while in the other sustained. In the crash of October 1987, it was the ever increasing concentration of automatically directed stock sales generated by the dynamic form of portfolio insurance that sent the market into its dizzying downward ride.

Chapter Five

CAN YOU BEAT THE MARKET? SHOULD YOU CARE?

For an individual facing the challenge of where and how to invest savings, even the mere thought of "beating the market" is valueless. It is our contention that for individual investors, the questions that should be asked are not "How can I (or you) beat the market?" but rather "What magnitude of returns do I want to aim for?" and "What magnitude of risk am I prepared to accept in order to achieve those returns?"

Who Beats the Market?

Lets's look at the opportunities, if any, for an individual investor to "beat the market." Professional managers are literally individual investors, and it might be best to look toward them and their track records for an indication of opportunities. "There is a handful of people who can beat the market in any one year," concedes Jeremy Grantham. "But how do you find them? Good performance has a negative correlation."[1] In other words, the manager who did well last year is more likely than average to do worse than average next year. We believe that while past performance need not be necessarily indicative of future *poor* performance, it is no guarantee whatever of future performance.

There is a reason for that: Investment is a dynamic business in which success almost automatically breeds future mediocrity. Everybody is watching what others do. If a technique works, others will use it too. Soon, whatever advantage is gained by using one method or system or philosophy will be available to others, which ultimately means no advantage at all.

Even when sophisticated computer models are devised that use all sorts of relevant information/criteria for picking stocks, and those models are then back-tested against past performance, the result is suspect. Though we can see how those stocks would have performed *with that system in place at the time*, it does not mean that if we put in place that model or system today, those stocks will perform that way from now on. In the near-mysterious way that the world (or at least the market) works, new criteria will come into

---

[1] Interview with Jeremy Grantham, op. cit.

play at just the moment we are installing our system that will render it fallible and irrelevant for the future.

Some portfolio managers do beat the market for a significant period of time. For example, the Mutual Shares Corporation, by focusing on unusual investments such as the securities of bankrupt companies, has compiled a record of superior performance over an extended period. However, if one examines a list of all funds produced by services that track mutual funds, pension funds and other institutional-type investment funds, one will see little consistency. Some members of any year's top ten performers may well have been among the bottom ten a year or five years before, while the top performers of those days may be at the bottom today.

Another myth that contributes to individuals believing they can beat the market is the perception that there are others "in the know" who are doing that. Perhaps, as investors, we are all somewhat seduced by the image of the professional trader standing in the middle of a futures trading pit or seated behind a multi-turreted trading desk with telephone receivers in each ear. We conclude that these people must be doing exceptionally well. Otherwise, why would they subject themselves to those conditions and behavior? Professional traders will explain success as stemming from their being "at one" with the market's excitement and thus able to sense its mood swings. The reality is that what market proximity really allows them to do (and standing in the pit is ultimate market proximity) is to observe: Who is making a move to do what? Which clerks are signalling to which brokers? Which brokers represent which firms? Knowing this, one can run in first and buy or sell in front of the order that experience tells you is about to unfold.

Under certain circumstances, such "front running" of orders actually may constitute a rules violation. An NYSE broker, having received a large order from a customer cannot, under the rules, execute for his own account in advance of executing for the customer. However, in the helter-skelter of futures and options trading pits, a trader may, in fact, get in front of a public customer's order, simply by observing what others around him or her are doing and then acting in front of *them*. In other words, the trader who appears to be doing very well often is cheating, with a small "c."

To approach one's personal investment goals and choices based on myths about how others are doing will, in all ways, lead to disappointment. Private asset allocation, based on a realistic appraisal of one's own risk/return needs, is the only sane way to proceed.

Asset Allocation and Personal Goals

Most investors can't afford to leave their funds alone to grow unmolested for a long period of time, say 15–20 years. The very factors that cause funds and stocks to decline in some years can also affect the investor's personal situation. In times of recessions, industrial restructurings, economic turmoil, political upheavals or contracting markets, people may lose their jobs or may have to make significant career changes. Then, too, life styles change: Serious health problems, divorces, having children—all these affect financial conditions. Funds set aside for long-term growth may be needed at precisely the time when the conditions that cause the need also shrink the investment. Or personal and family circumstances may require liquidation of investments during a period when it would be better to leave assets alone.

No longer the strategy of institutional investors alone, asset allocation has spread to the arena of the individual investor. It is viewed by many as the best, possibly the only, way of seeking returns while protecting against large reversals if one or two investments fail. Some investors use the strategy in managing their own monies; others hire professionals to allocate for them.

The asset categories through which the strategy can be applied also vary. Some investors directly diversify among stocks, Treasury bills, CD's, bonds and money market instruments; others add precious metals and/or real estate to the mix; others add international stocks and/or bonds; and still others may structure their portfolios among mutual funds that specialize in the different asset class investments. Finally, the proportions of the recipe itself vary widely, tailored as they must be to the individual needs of investors.

Over a period of time, certain asset classes have achieved certain rates of return. According to the 1988 Yearbook, *Stocks, Bonds, Bills and Inflation* (Chicago: Ibbotson Associates), the asset class that has performed the best during the past 62 years is stocks of small companies (with an average capitalization of $38 million). The average annual increase for this class has been 17.7 percent. A dollar invested in small company stocks at year-end 1925 grew to $1,202.97 by year-end 1987. This represents a compounded annual growth rate of 12.1 percent. The difference between average annual and compounded growth for this asset class has import for the investor. If each year's *actual* (rather than average) annual growth rate were 17.7 percent, then the compounded rate also would be 17.7 percent. But it isn't. In some years, the actual rate could be as high as 143 percent or as low as minus 51 percent while still resulting in an average annual rate of 17.7 percent. And that means that there have been wide swings in the price of this asset class from year-to-year, with high standard deviation. Thus, if one were able to hold onto these assets forever, they would prove to offer the best return; but due to the variability both of the results and investors' needs on a year-to-year basis, we cannot put all our eggs in this basket.

The asset class that offers the lowest average annual return is U.S. Treasury bills, with a return of 3.5 percent. The compounded growth rate for T-bills is also 3.5 percent, which means that this asset class has only nominal variability and low standard deviation. However, the price paid for this certainty is high: Since inflation has averaged 3.2 percent, investing in T-bills merely offers an opportunity (albeit a certain one) to keep up with inflation. T-bills then are at the other end of the spectrum from common stocks, offering the highest certainty but the least return.

In between the bookends of common stocks and T-bills are other asset classes with their varying degrees of certainty and reward. Table Nine (page 142) summarizes these. Choosing and apportioning investments among these assets classes is, in the end, dependent on one investor's personal situation, primarily his or her time-horizon. The investor must set for himself a time period during which funds can be invested and then left alone. This means facing and accepting his or her immediate, short-term and long-term cash requirements. For example, money set aside for school tuitions, or the purchase of a new home, or for reinvestment in one's own business carry implications for time-horizon and thus for the asset classes in which one should choose to invest. With these demands, an investor would be courting disaster were he to choose, say, small company stocks, which, as we have seen, can be subjected to a decline as great as minus 51.4 percent within one year. Even something as secure-sounding as long-term government bonds would carry too great a variability of return within one year (minus 9 percent) for the investor with these time-demands.

On the other hand, an investor with a very *long* time-horizon—say, one who has funds to be invested for retirement—has the luxury of being able to ride through interim adverse results aiming for a future higher growth rate. Since 1926, there has never been a

20-year period in which common stocks did not produce a positive compounded annual return. In fact, starting from the end of WWII, the *lowest* compound annual return achieved during any 20-year period was 6.5 percent (for the years 1959-1978), which is considerably higher than the 3.5 percent produced by T-bills. Our long-time-horizon investor would be foolish not to choose the common stocks over the T-bills.

How do you determine your own personal time-horizon? Obviously, there's no one mathematical equation that produces a right or wrong answer for each individual. But there is a self-scrutiny that must occur, and perhaps a five-year time-horizon is a good starting benchmark. During most five-year periods one is likely to have experienced (or witnessed) the following: one or more job changes, one or more house moves, a birth or death, a new school situation for one or more family members, a change in health or medical situation. A five-year period also usually will have witnessed one or more economic cycles in the life of the country.

With a five-year time-horizon, and a subsequent notion of the amount of risk one can accept, the investor will be able to decide: What kind of returns am I free enough to aim for? The result is a personal strategic asset allocation plan, something that will stay in place for some designated period of time.

Even the largest corporations, with enormous pools of retirement assets, go through a self-examination process similar to the one outlined here, in order to determine strategic asset allocation. Consultants and actuarial firms are hired to conduct studies and make extraordinarily complex projections about retirement, health, mortality, and other factors that will determine asset allocation strategies. A lot of time, money, and computer power is expended, and the result is typically an answer that says pension funds should be invested 60 percent in stocks and 40 percent in bonds. Oddly enough, this evolved answer of 60/40 is probably a pretty good rule of thumb to follow for most private investors with a five-year time-horizon. Though able to aim for very long-term results, the modern corporation faces political and interim bottom-line realities that have the effect of rendering its time and risk considerations similar to those of the individual investor with a five-year horizon.

Does putting into place a strategic asset allocation plan mean forgoing all further interest in the stock market and other asset groups? The answer is no. An investor must be able to say, "I have a strategic plan, but at various times there may be reasons for evaluating that one asset class is about to go up and another go down." The strategic plan is a long-term plan of asset allocation that makes no prediction as to what next year will bring; yet there are events and decisions in the life of the market that *will* affect what next year brings. To some extent, these occurrences should be taken into account, with the result that *tactical asset allocation* is brought into play.

Tactical asset allocation is based on changes in the predictions about asset characteristics. Should interest rates suddenly rise, for example, bond prices are likely

141

Table Nine

Series	Geometric Mean	Arithmetic Mean	Standard Deviation	Distribution
Common Stocks	9.9%	12.0%	21.1%	
Small Company Stocks	12.1	17.7	35.9	
Long-Term Corporate Bonds	4.9	5.2	8.5	
Long-Term Government Bonds	4.3	4.6	8.5	
Intermediate-Term Government Bonds	4.8	4.9	5.5	
U.S. Treasury Bills	3.5	3.5	3.4	
Inflation Rates	3.0	3.2	4.8	

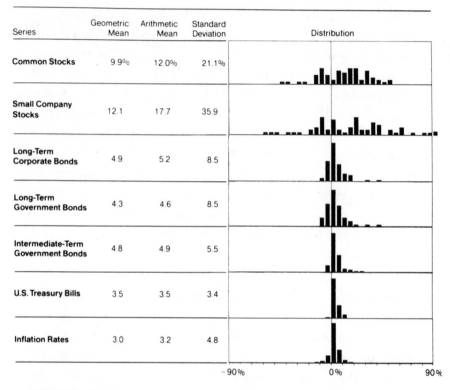

−90% 0% 90%

SOURCE: SBBI (Stocks, Bonds, Bills and Inflation) 1988 Yearbook (Chicago: Ibbotson Associates, 1988).

to drop. This event will then change predictions about the performance of bonds as an asset class and to *some extent* should be taken into consideration. We stress "some extent" because it's our view that tactical asset allocation should not move an investor away from his or her strategic asset allocation strategy but rather should be merely one element causing the investor to shift his or her asset mix temporarily and only slightly. Giving credence to this approach should not be seen as countenancing the technique known as *market timing*, by which one gets in and out of markets based on bets about which asset classes will go up or down tomorrow.

Market Timing

Market timing seldom works. Among those most hurt by the October 19 crash were market timers. "The signals that market timers rely on are based on a change in trends and they are supposed to make investors aware of a trend in time for investors to act," noted a post-crash article in the *AAII Journal*.[2] Investors who try to get in and out on every "signal" seldom make money, especially after paying transaction costs and taxes. They also run the real risk of being constantly whipsawed, trading themselves out of positions that would be profitable if held over the long term. As John Maynard Keynes said: "Most of those who attempt to, sell too late and buy too late, and do both too often, incurring heavy expenses."

When it comes to stocks, there are many classic indicators (or signals) cited by market analysts as reasons for quickly moving in or out of the market for specific stocks.

---

[2] Maria Crawford Scott, "The October Crash: Who Was Hurt the Most—And Why," AAII Journal, January 1988, pp. 17–18.

(1) Is management selling stocks?

(2) Has the short interest (the number of shares that are sold short) climbed from a low to a substantial percentage of the outstanding stock?

(3) Is volume greater when the stock goes down than when it goes up?

(4) Do put options greatly outnumber call options? All these, say market timing specialists, are substantive reasons for entering or exiting from an investment in a company's stock. The fact is that there can be many reasons for each of these four indicators (and for countless other so-called signals) that have little bearing on whether a stock will go up or down.

Are inside managers selling because they lack confidence in the future of the company they run? Or is it because they need cash for college fees, must exercise options before they expire, are about to leave the company for another job, or simply wish to "balance" their personal portfolios? And how old are those figures anyway? Insider trading figures go to the SEC and generally do not become really public for 30 days or so. A post-crash *Wall Street Journal* article noted: "Like most stock market indicators, the practice of tracking sales and purchases by corporate insiders failed miserably at predicting the October 19 crash."[3]

---

[3] *Wall Street Journal*, January 19, 1988, p. 31.

Is the short interest high because investors expect the stock to decline in the near future? That's the common interpretation. But a high short interest is also something of a safety net for a stock. Also, how did that short-interest build up—suddenly or over a significant period? Is there in fact a manipulation of sorts going on, especially in high-multiple, thinly traded small-company stocks where the shorts' selling drives down the price so that the shorts can profit? How exposed are the shorts? Are they susceptible to a squeeze if the stock continues to appreciate even a little bit? Will they perhaps support the stock as they rush to cover on any decline rather than be a harbinger of significant and long-term decline? And again, how old are those short-interest figures? In today's market, how real are the figures? Index arbitrageurs often sell short huge blocks of stock as part of the arbitrage strategy. These short sales inflate the figures but say nothing at all about investor sentiment concerning those stocks.

As for the flow of money into or out of a stock as indicated by the so-called on-balance volume—the trading volume as a function of the direction and size of price movement—it could be cyclical, or evidence of disinterest rather than dislike, or reflect the activities of a few large investors rather than many smaller ones.

Paradoxically, some of these indicators can be read both ways, pushing for either a buy *or* a sell of a specific stock. This merely proves our point: Market timing offers no way to beat the market. Tactical asset allocation, on the other hand, though ostensibly a timing approach, offers a balanced view for combining changes in predictions with an already established strategic asset allocation plan.

Tactical Asset Allocation

Short-term tactical asset allocation is based on buying undervalued assets that offer greater than normal returns. Its popularity has grown significantly since October 1987, in part as a direct result of the events of that month. In August 1987, an estimated $27 billion was managed by asset allocators; by September 1988, the number had grown to $38.3 billion.[4]

Using various methods based on different types of projections, tactical asset allocation promotes buying and selling among asset classes according to projections as to which asset classes will perform best over the short run. The projections usually are founded on a view of what constitutes normal market returns (unlike portfolio insurance, which, as we have seen, is based on an exaggerated view) and so the effect of tactical asset allocation is to contribute to reduced swings in the market rather than increased volatility. The traditional asset classes switched among are stocks, bonds, and cash equivalents, though lately real estate, gold, foreign stocks and foreign bonds have been added to the mix by several more aggressive money-management firms.

---

[4] *Pensions & Investment Age*, September 5, 1988, p. 1, "Tactical Allocation Soars."

From an investor's point of view, implementing tactical asset allocation means acting only when you think a certain asset class has deviated from what you believe is its fair or normal value. For example, in the summer of 1982, just prior to the beginning of the bull market rally, the dividend yields from common stocks looked as if they would reach between 5 1/2 percent and 6 percent for the year. (Yields are the dividends divided by the stocks prices; when yields are low you must pay more for the stocks while receiving the same or less returns than where yields are high.) If that projection turned out to be an accurate one, that would be the highest one-year yield than for any one year in the previous 25 years. The summer of 1982, in other words, appeared to be a good time to buy common stocks.

Under tactical asset allocation, an investor would have shifted funds somewhat within his long-range strategic asset allocation plan so as to put a greater emphasis on common stocks. By the beginning of 1987, however, dividend yields on common stocks looked as though they'd reach a low of 3 percent for that year. That was a good time to sell stocks, and the tactical asset allocator would have shifted the proportion of common stocks in his or her portfolio to reflect that projection.

But not all asset classes move in isolation, and there are moments when tactical asset allocation strategies advise shifting to more than one asset class simultaneously. The summer of 1982 was a good time to buy stocks, but not at the expense of long-term government bonds, for instance. Current yields on bonds were in excess of 13 percent, which meant bonds offered a greater income yield than at any time ever before. It was a good time to buy bonds, as well.

It was not, however, a good moment to be buying Treasury bills. From the late 1970's up until mid-1982, returns on cash (which are the yields on T-bills) had been extraordinarily high. Double-digit levels of inflation (often associated with a super-heated economy) had led many investors to put their assets in cash or cash equivalents—short-term investments that will pay out before inflation can take its cost. But by 1982, those adjustments to the economy that had to be made in order to reduce inflation (higher interest rates and higher unemployment chief among them) were beginning to have their desired effect: the economy gradually was slowing down. This meant that inflation would soon decline, and *that* meant that the yields on T-bills also would decline. In 1982, then, the tactical asset allocator would have been shifting his or her portfolio mix away from cash and more towards common stocks and long-term government bonds.

We again emphasize "shifting away from" or "shifting towards" and not "replacing" or "substituting" one asset class with another. Tactical asset allocation is an often a successful strategy when used as part of one's overall long-term strategic asset allocation plan. It is not market timing, or any other quick in-and-out, all-or-nothing method for beating the market. It is a short-term way of rebalancing emphasis within one's portfolio based on reasonable projections about how one or more asset classes will perform.

Tactical asset allocation, as employed by billion-dollar money managers, often is built on highly complex models. But ordinary investors can find the basic statistics that we believe are the critical indicators of asset class performance in the daily newspaper. Knowing yields for common stocks, current yields on long-term government bonds, and T-bill rates (a proxy for inflation as we have illustrated) is sufficient for making decisions about these asset classes and the weight they should take up within one's portfolio over the short run.

Investing the Equity Portion of Your Portfolio

If one subscribes to the investment plan described here—using overall strategic asset allocation with short-term tactical asset allocation shifts—the investor is likely to always have a significant part of his or her portfolio in common stocks. Neither strategic asset allocation nor short-term tactical asset allocation have any advice to offer on *which* common stocks to buy and when to buy or sell them.

There are compelling arguments that the personal investor always should maintain a diversified stock portion of one's portfolio, and we have outlined these in Chapter Two on indexing. But if you want to have more fun, there are two ways to do it.

The traditional method is to create a unique portfolio (unique to you, that is) of individual issues. By doing this, you've added an element of risk into the portfolio as a tradeoff for a chance at higher return. As we saw in Chapter Two, the conceptual way of approaching this challenge is to look at the efficient curve frontier, which offers an exact representation of that tradeoff. For example, we might select 10 stocks, all of which have a historical beta of 2 and be fairly confident that if the market moves upward, that the gain in our portfolio will significantly outpace the market's gain. Intuitively though, one can see that this is an inefficient way to proceed: How do we know we picked the right 10 stocks with a beta of 2? Since the chances for the actual beta to behave differently from the estimated beta are quite high, our selections might come in at a much lower beta than we had estimated. In that case, we would have taken considerable risk, and the market would have moved favorably, but we would not have benefitted as much as we had intended for the degree of risk taken.

Another way to "play" with the stock portion of your portfolio is to buy the entire market. The optimal portfolio of risks is, in fact, the entire market. Once you've bought the entire market you've obtained the maximum benefit of diversification while giving up the least possible return. If you *really* want to play, though, which means taking added risk over the market's normal risk, consider buying the whole market by leveraging. Leveraging entails borrowing money (i.e., not having to use your own) to increase the size of the assets you own.

Let's say your portfolio is $1 million, in which you've determined that approximately $700,000 is to be in common stocks, $200,000 in long-term bonds, and $100,000 in cash equivalents. You're also assuming that the stock market will turn in a typical performance for the coming year of plus 12 percent. If you wished to try to do better than 12 percent (or make more than $87,500) you could either select a portfolio of a limited number of stocks and aim for making $168,000 or you could borrow $700,000 and buy $1.4 million worth of stock. (We'll ignore interest costs for simple illustrative purposes at this point.) If you had bought $1.4 million worth of stock and the market went up the expected 12 percent, you would have accomplished the same thing as if you had chosen route one, the limited number of stocks, and doubled the market's performance.

Using Derivative Instruments: Futures

One efficient way of buying the entire market and using whatever leverage factor you want is to buy 10 futures contracts—in particular, the most active futures contract, the S&P 500. At current writing, one future is equal to about $140,000 worth of stock. So ten futures is $1.4 million of stock. If you've bought the futures and the market then goes up 12 percent, you make $168,000 in your stocks for a 24 percent return on the portion of the total portfolio that is allocated to stocks. Again, this would be the equivalent in gain of having picked successfully ten stocks that behaved with a beta of 2—in other words, stocks that performed twice as well as the market.

Let's scrutinize more precisely what our hypothetical $1 million portfolio looks like. To begin, as we have said, our portfolio allocation will be 70 percent in stock, 20 percent in long-term bonds and 10 percent in cash equivalents (say, 90-day T-bills). One of the features of the futures contract is that it does not employ cash but rather merely requires posting margin. Thus the $700,000 that we've allocated to stocks can be employed as additional investment in cash equivalents, the lowest-risk asset class. Our hypothetical portfolio, then, will have $800,000 of T-bills: the $100,000 initially invested in cash equivalents plus the $700,000 allocated to stock but not consumed by it. You would not want to put that $700,000 into another asset class, such as long-term bonds, because you have already decided how much bond-owning risk you are willing to accept. Of course, by owning the futures contracts instead of the actual stocks, you will not receive the dividends paid on those common stocks. Instead, you will receive the income on the extra $700,000 of T-bills. Most of the time, the income on those T-bills will be greater than the dividends foregone. However, the marketplace gives recognition to that fact and most likely will require you to pay a premium on your futures contract (the amount over the cash market that the future sells for) that is equal to the amount of extra T-bill earnings over dividends. If you had the good fortune to have bought your futures contract at less than the full premium, you will have captured arbitrage profit. (Any investor is able to obtain from a broker the exact calculation for the premium.)

The portfolio that we've constructed will be easy to manage and maintain. To review, it contains $700,000 of 90-day T-bills, which will have to be repurchased four times a year as the last issue expires. This is a nearly costless transaction for which a broker normally will charge only a nominal service fee (you can also buy directly from the government and pay *no* charge whatsoever). The portfolio also contains $200,000 of long-term government bonds; these simply sit in your account for anywhere from 20 to 30 years collecting coupons. And, thirdly, you will have five futures contracts. These will have to be renewed at each expiration: in March, June, September, and December. (One can always try to jump ahead and renew one expiration further along, but the pricing mechanism for more than one expiration ahead is poor and should not be counted on.) The cost of buying a futures contract for the individual investor would be approximately $50 per contract: $25 for the initiation of the position and $25 for its reversal or expiration. Our theoretical portfolio, you can see, might face a cost of no more than $1,000 per year, which is five futures × $50 × four times a year.

It will also be a simple matter to make changes in this portfolio. Suppose you've decided to reduce your stock exposure from 70 percent of your portfolio down to 56 percent and to build up your cash-equivalent position accordingly. All you have to do is call your broker and tell him or her to sell out one futures contract. You don't have to buy any more T-bills because you already own them. In addition, were you the kind of investor seeking a higher-risk stock portfolio (say, with a beta of two), you merely will purchase an additional five futures. At the time of this writing, the margin requirement on an S&P 500 futures contract is $20,000. With 10 futures, you'd now have a margin requirement of $200,000, which is more than covered by the $800,000 of T-bills and $200,000 of long-term bonds in your portfolio.

Futures contracts also exist for long-term bonds, so this same simple portfolio structure also lends itself to efficient changes in allocating more assets to bonds. Usually, yields on long-term bonds are greater than yields on T-bills. Therefore, you can expect to buy a bond future at a discount from the cash market for bonds. At present, one Treasury bond future is equivalent to approximately $90,000 worth of bonds. If you call your broker and say, "sell one stock future and buy one bond future," in effect, you will be changing your portfolio mix from 70-20-10 to 56-29-15, (stock, long-term bonds, and cash, respectively).

It should be apparent from the above description that while futures are generally considered to be risky instruments because of the degree of leverage that one can obtain (for example, $140,000 of stock exposure on only $20,000 of margin, a 7-to-1 leverage), you need not necessarily use that much leverage. In theory, you can use no leverage at all. In fact, the portfolio we've described, using five futures, employs no leverage, because the $700,000 of T-bills is there to support the $700,000 of stocks exposure.

At this point, some would-be investors with particular interests in stocks might find our hypothetical portfolio boring. For such investors, there *are* other future contracts that can be drawn on. We'll here cite three in particular: (1) the future on the New York Stock Exchange Index; (2) the future on the Value Line Index; and (3) the future on the Major Market Index. None of these futures have the same liquidity in their trading marketplaces as do the S&P 500 futures. There just aren't that many interested buyers and sellers. Therefore, these will be more expensive instruments to use. When you buy, you'll pay an extra premium; and when you sell, you are likely to receive a discount from the full premium. But they *do* offer the opportunity to put to the test one's investment ideas or theories, while still remaining within the structural framework of asset allocation that we recommend.

For example, if you hold the view that large capitalization stocks (stocks of America's largest corporations) are a more propitious investment, at a given moment, than other stocks, you could buy the future on the Major Market Index (which is made up of 20 Dow Jones Industrial Average-type stocks). On the other hand, the future on the Value Line Index offers greater exposure to investment in small stocks, and if you hold decided views about the prospects for small-cap companies, you might want to buy *that* future. The returns for small capitalization stocks have been superior to that of larger capitalization stocks, although the risk of owning those stocks is considerably greater.

At this point, it should be apparent that we do not see room for much profit to be made by investors selecting their own portfolios of individual securities. Hypothetically, an investor can learn everything that is in the public record about a targeted company and its industry, can monitor the progress of both, and be alert to outside factors that might affect outcome. But even then, we doubt that any investor can consistently identify and predict such factors or even be able to prognosticate the way in which they might affect the investment. Besides, no matter how well-informed or successfully predictive an investor may be, the simple fact remains that most of what happens to a stock's price is because of what is happening to the stock market and not the details of what is happening to that one company or even its industry.

The individual investor with a portfolio of a few select stocks does not escape the market. Stocks fluctuate in tune with the overall market as well as in response to their own dynamics. Various studies have indicated that anywhere from 40 percent to 50 percent of a stock's movement can be attributed to market forces in general and 10 percent to 15 percent to the influence of the industry to which it belongs. The unique characteristics of the company itself account for only a small percentage. Other factors, which no one has identified, account for anywhere from 15 percent to 20 percent of the price movement. Admittedly, these figures cover a broad range, but they do agree on the central point: The market itself is the major influence on stock price movements. And no investor escapes its movements.

It should then follow rather conclusively that if you are going to be subjected to the ups and downs of the market, you're better off investing in the entire market at the start. It is in the end, much more profitable to shift broad assets within a portfolio based on strategic asset allocation with tactical shorter-term adjustments than it is to "pick stocks."

Chapter Six ————————————————

COMPUTERS AND ELECTRONIC COMMUNICATIONS AS FINANCIAL TOOLS

Information drives the stock market, and there is more of it than ever before. In the modern world, the means by which this information is processed and disseminated throughout the marketplace is through a communications system that is computer- and electronically based. The question now must arise in our analysis of the changing stock market: Does the greater amount of information and the speed with which it can be disseminated create a condition in which market participants, in their haste to act on "quick" information, trigger sharp price swings? Or are we receiving sizeable benefits and rewards from the quick processing of greater amounts of information?

Information Drives the Stock Market

The power of information is proved constantly. Perhaps Wall Street's favorite story is set in 1815, during the Battle of Waterloo. At one point in the fighting it appeared that the English were going to lose this decisive battle. News of the dismal outlook reached the London financial markets by ship and runner within a few days. Bond prices plunged as investors crowded the doors in an effort to escape the certain collapse of the British Empire. Meanwhile, though, after the couriers left the front with the bad news, the tide of battle had turned, and Napoleon's forces were crushed.

Baron Nathan de Rothschild, a member of the European banking family, was camped somewhere behind the British lines when he learned that the British had Napoleon on the run. Somehow (by fast ship and courier, the report has it) the Baron got the updated news to his partners in London 12 hours ahead of everyone else. The Rothschilds were able to scoop up the British bonds at bargain prices from investors still in the grip of panic from the first, inaccurate news reports. A few hours later, when the rest of the market learned that Napoleon had been defeated, bond prices soared, and the Rothschilds pocketed a huge instant fortune.

Also in the 1800s, Julius Reuter used carrier pigeons to ferry stock prices from Brussels to Paris, closing a gap in the early telegraph network. His birds proved faster than the trains and therefore more valuable. When the increasing efficiency of the telegraph rendered his pigeons obsolete, Reuter moved his operation to London and continued to supply clients with financial news by telegraph. Thus began the Reuters News Agency, one of the leading suppliers of financial news in the world.

Dow Jones, which publishes the most popular financial news service, began in an equally prosaic way. Young men were hired to copy stock market news and gossip items with styluses onto sandwiches made up of sheets of thin paper collated with sheets of carbon. The finished product, just one page long, was then rushed to subscribers around Wall Street by foot messengers. Later, Dow Jones switched to electric ticker machines, the ancestors of today's electronic wire service, which professional investors rely on for timely market news and data and which even individual investors can access on their home computers.

How Computers Are Used by Brokers and Traders

For the securities markets to work effectively, it is essential that the brokerage community and the exchange facilities all work effectively. Up through the early 1960s, a busy day on the Big Board saw ten million shares change hands. Between two and three million shares traded on an ordinary day. During the next 20 to 25 years the number of individual stockholders doubled to almost 50 million, as many new companies were formed and issued stock. Stock prices rose, and existing companies declared splits, increasing the number of shares available to trade. On the NYSE the average number of shares listed reached 65.7 billion by 1987, up from 11.3 billion 20 years previously.

In 1975, the era of fixed commissions ended and discounting began, making it cheaper to trade than before. In April 1975 the typical institutional investor was paying 26 cents per share commission. By 1986, the rate was down to 7.5 cents. For the individual investor the end of the fixed commissions had mixed results: Some of the full-service brokers actually were able to raise their rates, but the availability of discount brokers created the opportunity for most investors to realize a large reduction in commission rates. Coincidental with the reduction in commission rates, the NYSE experienced a sharp increase in the turnover of listed shares. By 1987, the turnover rate hit 73 percent, up from 21 percent in 1975. As a consequence, reported volume reached 47.8 billion shares during 1987.

Throughout the period of the 1970s and the 1980s, institutional investors played an increasingly dominant role in the trading of stocks. The sharpest indication of this trend has been the percentage of volume accounted for by large block transactions—10,000 shares or more. In 1987, that percentage reached 51.7 percent, compared to only 15.4 percent in 1970. The private investor has, by his or her own actions, substantially given up the opportunity to *directly* own stocks, often by virtue of the growth of pension plans which has handed over the investment process to a third partner. According to NYSE surveys, the percentage of individual investors owning shares in NYSE companies dropped from 80.9 percent in 1982 to 69.7 percent in 1985. During that same period, the percentage owning mutual funds jumped from 15.6 percent to 30.3 percent. By the beginning of 1987 pension plans controlled over 20 percent of the market value of all equities. As we have suggested earlier, the growing institutionalization of the stock market has been a huge factor in the growing usage of program trading techniques.

In 1970, average daily trading volume on the NYSE was 11 million shares. The first day that more than 100 million shares traded was August 18, 1982, marking, along with the prior day's rally, the start of a bull market. Just two years later, volume surpassed 200 million shares a day. And a little more than three years after that, on the day of the crash, more than 600 million shares changed hands. (The NYSE computer systems, which some thought had been overbuilt for handling up to 400-million-share days, choked on the volume but somehow managed to keep humming.) Volume settled back after October 19 to an average of about 175 million shares a day although it dropped as low as 90 million shares in August 1988.

The inescapable fact is that the organizational effort required to handle the movement of hundreds of millions of shares of stock could not even have been imagined in the pre-computer era. The informational requirements alone astound: How much of what was purchased at what price? At what price was it sold and to whom? Has it been paid for or not? In the financial industry, the industry itself is the largest customer for this information about itself. In the end, the effectiveness with which the securities industry performs all its functions, from maintaining customer accounts to executing trades, affects the prices at which trades occur. In a climate of operational inefficiency—one in which there are errors on trades, the buy and sell sides of a trade go unreconciled, or payments for securities are delayed—traders and portfolio managers eventually withdraw from trading or making buy and sell decisions.

One can also argue that without the electronic mechanisms capable of tracking the often multifarious actions of both large and small players in the marketplace, such abuses as insider-information trading would be more rampant than they are now and less easily corrected. There is simply no end to the importance of the computer as Wall Street's major administrative tool. Probably the ultimate manifestation of the computer as the administrative tool has been the fact that shares of stock in their basic paper form rarely change hands anymore. With stocks moving from seller to buyer through the mechanism of electronic book transfer, rare is the investor who actually takes possession of a stock certificate.

But the computer had other uses to which it might be put. And when Wall Street discovered that computers made it possible to, first, look at and, then, rearrange data in new, more useful ways, it was simply a matter of time before blinking screens appeared on every desk. Before long, computer terminals were providing traders and analysts with up-to-the-second market information from services such as Quotron, Bridge, NASDAQ, Instinct, Dow Jones, Reuters, Shark, Telerate, and Telestock, to mention only several vendors of market services.

This avalanche of numbers would have been useless to the time-pressured trader without some sort of organizational system that could be applied. Software developers came up with techniques for sorting and analyzing data in ways the traders could quickly absorb. Today, a major news development on the Dow Jones News Service is announced with a series of beeps indicating its importance. A single screen on a trader's desk can plot on a vertical scale the constantly changing spread between the S&P 500 Index futures and the cash index. Another screen presents side-by-side, in the form of tables of numbers, the minute-by-minute changes in the Dow Industrials, the S&P 500, and the S&P 100. The terminal can alert the trader when certain spreads appear or when one of these indices passes through a significant level. In an instant, the trader can see where the markets stand, both on their own and in relation to each other.

Computers now track and store virtually every bit of information generated by the financial markets. And, in the last 30 years, there has come to exist more information generated about more aspects of more companies than ever before. Brokers and traders use computers to process two major types of information: information about the fundamentals of companies and information about stock and index prices.

Fundamental information today exists in differing modes: financial data required by the SEC; detailed research constantly being done by investment analysts; data bases of fundamental facts about companies, collected by others, as well as immediate news releases issued by companies about themselves; and instantly computer-summoned historical summaries of all such news releases.

Market and price information also has multiplied over the past two decades. Prices can be constantly tracked and instantly disseminated throughout the marketplace. Market volume, bids and asked, up and down movements—all are accessible at a moment's notice in present and historical terms.

Figure Eight is of a SHARK Service Stock Summary[1] to which any person with a personal computer can subscribe.

The summary displays current and historical technical trading data for a particular stock, in this case Wang. Price category includes current closing, and

[1] For information, write Wang Financial Information Service Corp., 120 Wall Street, New York, NY 10005.

WAN/B — STOCK SUMMARY — PAGE: 1/2

WAN/B	TODAY	05/26	05/25	05/24	05/23	05/22	20 DAY	50 DAY	150 DAY
Price	8	8 1/8	8	8 1/4	8 1/2	8 1/2	8 3/8	8 1/4	8 5/8
Rel Px	.995	1.008	.970	.968	1.011	.969	1.000	.996	.999
High	8 1/8	8 1/8	8 3/8	8 1/2	8 1/2	8 3/4	8 7/8	9 1/8	10 3/8
Low	8	8	8	8 1/4	8 3/8	8 1/2	7 1/2	7 1/4	7 1/4
Blk P/D	0/0	0/0	0/.13	.13/.13	0/0	0/.13	.14/.13	.13/.14	.13/.13
Lqdty	168	119	93	62	152	153	178	186	183
TrdSize	1,977	1,783	2,508	1,589	1,136	2,368	2,323	3,062	2,915
Volume	168	119	280	124	152	307	409	381	395
%Blocks	54	28	63	38	0	51	47	54	52
#Blocks	4	2	9	3	0	6	8	8	8
%Up/%Dn	0/0	0/0	0/11	33/67	0/0	0/33	10/23	11/21	11/15
%SmBlks	4	22	9	20	12	19	11	12	12
#SmBlks	1	4	4	4	3	9	8	6	5
%Up/%Dn	0/0	25/25	0/0	0/25	0/33	0/22	12/17	14/12	15/12
%NoBlks	42	50	28	41	88	30	42	35	36
#NoBlks	80	61	99	71	131	115	153	113	107
%Up/%Dn	3/4	3/2	7/8	15/15	19/18	10/8	13/12	13/13	12/12

Wang Financial Information Services Network Service ONLINE

WAN/B
N R

(pg x) 15:33:38 89/ 5/30

Figure Eight

average prices of the stock for 20-, 50-, and 150-day periods. "Rel Px" means the relative price of the stock, calculated by dividing the stock's change since the previous close by the change in the S&P 500 index. "High" indicates the highest price for the day or period; and "low" the lowest price for the day or period. "Blk P/D" gives the average premium and discount on block trades (10,000 shares or more) in relation to previous trades. "Lqdty" means liquidity, or the average number of shares needed to move the stock price by 1/8. "Trd Size" is the average trade size, arrived at by taking the total volume for the day divided by the number of trades. "Volume" is the daily or average trading volume. "% Blocks" is that percent of total volume that was traded in blocks (10,000 shares or more); and "# Blocks" is the daily or average number of trades.

Within seconds, then, this one screen sheet provides complete information as to the size, scope, price, and activity of a given stock, with added relative and historical perspectives as well. Before computers, this kind of information would have taken analysts hours if not days to compile and arrange, by which time it would have lost its usefulness.

The sum total of all this information is the price at which any investment product, be it a stock or a bond or an index or an option, trades at a given point in time. The more accurate information the system can acquire, absorb, process and correctly interpret, the more efficient the markets become at pricing each asset. The reverse holds true as well. Inefficiencies in collecting information and getting it where it belongs result in the kinds of opportunities the Rothschilds enjoyed in 1815, although rarely on such a scale or magnitude. Even administrative information can affect the prices of investments. Brokerage firms must keep close tabs on the value of their inventories of stocks, bonds and other financial instruments: the firm's capital requirements to support its operations, customer data, who owes what to whom, what trades have been made and in what form. What the brokerage industry does, and how well it does it, has an impact on the prices at which trades take place.

Liquidity—the ease, speed and orderliness with which trades can take place—is everything, and it requires instant knowledge of supply and demand, what trades have taken place and at what price. In the globalized markets, such details are as essential to efficient pricing as the auction itself. At the time of this writing, the New York Mercantile Exchange and the Chicago Mercantile Exchange (the second largest futures market) are considering linking their markets via a worldwide computer network called Globex. Globex would provide for 24-hour electronic trading in such commodities futures as stock indexes, T-bills, foreign currencies, crude oil and other energy products, cattle, hogs, and pork bellies among others. Traditional auction methods would continue to operate during the exchange's regular trading hours, but after the close, the Globex network would take over, enabling futures traders anywhere in the world to punch in bids and asks (offers to buy and offers to sell) and have them matched up electronically.

Although the exchanges expect this linkage to bring an enormous increase in the volume of futures trading and thus expanded liquidity for the markets in those commodities, we are not convinced of its efficacy. We recognize the need for globalization of the marketplace but doubt that, in this instance, traders will retire from the auction leaving their bids and asks overnight in an electronic system, where they can be "picked off" by other traders. Still, the markets have come a long way from the days when traders passed around slips of paper under a buttonwood tree on the banks of the Hudson River.

How Money Managers Use Computers

Perhaps the computer's most valuable use is in the investment process itself, for it is in *that* realm that quantum leaps have been made in the application of information for the purpose of making money.

Techniques of financial analysis applied to individual stocks (as we saw in Chapters Three and Four) have been around for a long time. Even the most sophisticated analysts, however, whether they used fundamental or technical analysis, or both, were ultimately coming up with conclusions that applied to one stock, a couple of stocks or, in some cases, one industry. There are still analysts who use those methods today, and there are still many money managers who base their buying and selling decisions on those analysts' recommendations. But that is yesterday's stock market, and it is a fading one. As we have shown throughout this book, those methods are being discarded by today's sophisticated investors because, ultimately, they do not work. They do not "beat the market" and on the isolated occasions when they do, the returns generated do not justify the risk taken.

Today's stock market has changed because now quantitative analytic techniques can be applied to hundreds or thousands of stocks, which can then be bought and sold in aggregates. That is program trading, and it is the computer that has made it all possible. The ease with which the computer can sift through and evaluate the enormous amount of information about companies that is now available makes quantitative analysis readily operative for billion-dollar money managers. Thousands of companies can be analyzed using a wide variety of models; comparisons then can be made with other stocks using the chosen model as a basis for the comparison; and rankings can be made of all the stocks, on the basis of the comparisons. Finally, computer programs are created that will explore huge data bases and make stock selection using the system developed from the model of analysis.

Steps like these have become the *modus operandi* of today's billion-dollar fund managers, and the reader should realize that many of these computer programs are very complex indeed and way beyond the reach of the individual private investor. Their workings are nonetheless important to understand, because their use has changed the stock market—indeed, now dominates it—and that fact alone has significant ramifications for all investors.

The Geewax, Terker Model

The more sophisticated systems are based on a two-part quantitative model: the identification of expected return, founded on information about the fundamentals of a company; and the measurement of riskiness, based on stock price behavior.

Geewax, Terker and Associates, a firm based in Phoenixville, Pennsylvania, with $3 billion under management, developed such a model and uses it to pick the stocks it buys for its institutional clients from a universe of 3,000 stocks. The model produces a ranking of stocks from the dual perspectives of expected return and required return (or risk).

Expected return is defined as the projected future price of a stock, and this projection is derived from the model's analysis of company fundamentals, a resultant earnings forecast, and price/earnings (p/e) predictions. The model reaches deep down into a company's balance statement and looks at such specifics as receivables and payables to assess its corporate cash flow for a given period. Geewax, Terker focuses on corporate cash flow for current period ended as a good forecaster of what earnings a company will report over the following one or two quarters.

The system next analyzes p/e ratios by looking at trends in inflationary expectations as evidenced by Treasury bill rates (as we've seen, a common standard for inflation measurement). By multiplying earnings times the p/e ratio, the model arrives at a price objective for the company. That price objective is then compared to the current price of the stock, and an *expected return* for a certain moment in time is established.

You can see already how essential the computer is to even this first step of the process. The traditional money manager may be receiving the best analysis of the Street, but still can't possibly produce earnings forecasts for all the stocks worth considering. There are other, albeit less thorough, ways to approach this task, however. One could subscribe to a service that, by using *its* computer, provides earnings estimates. Figure Nine is of one page from such a service—Zacks Estimate Service's *Current Consensus 12/30/88* report, a compilation of earnings estimates made by brokerage analysts.[2]

One might conceivably accept these estimates as one's defined expected return and then proceed to somehow establish a price objective and arrive at some measurement of volatility or riskiness in the price behavior. But both those assessments would be difficult to make without the aid of a computer, to say nothing of the important final stage, which is to come up

---

[2] Zacks Investment Research, Inc., Zacks Estimate Service, *Current Consensus 12/30/88*, p. 41.

with a ranking of stocks that tells you how to invest. For systems like Geewax, Terker's, by contrast, the combination of these analytic insights with a main-frame computer takes three hours.

The second half of the Geewax, Terker model is the analysis of how much risk there is in a stock's situation, called its *required return*. The model defines risk as the probability that the return actually realized may differ from the expected return originally projected. Stock price behavior is analyzed to measure that probability, and risk is factored in on a relative basis, through comparisons of company and industry factors for various stocks (how General Motors compares with IBM; how stocks within the same industry compare).

To have a sense of how massive the computer operation and processing can become, note that the Geewax, Terker model has, as merely *one* of its small parts, a program that determines which stock prices have been acting like which other stock prices over a specified period of time. Its goal is to be able to locate stocks whose price action seems predictable under similar conditions. The computer has in its memory a graph or matrix built of the 3,000 stocks on the vertical and the same 3,000 stocks on the horizontal, creating a field of three million "cells." Within each of these cells the computer compares the price of the particular stock for the past 52 weeks against the price of every one of the other 2,999 stocks for the same period. When the price behavior of two stocks is found to be similar, the computer does a further screen to see what other characteristics they might share, and to see if this similarity

CONSENSUS OF BROKERAGE ANALYSTS EPS ESTIMATES

COMPANY	LAST FSC YEAR — YEAR ENDED	LAST FSC YEAR — ACTUAL EPS ($)	NEXT QUARTER — TO REPT	NEXT QUARTER — MEAN EST ($)	CURRENT FISCAL YEAR — MEAN ESTIMATE ($)	CURRENT FISCAL YEAR — STAND DEV ($)	CURRENT FISCAL YEAR — NUMBER ESTIMATES	CURRENT FISCAL YEAR — CHANGE MEAN (%)	NEXT FISCAL YEAR — MEAN ESTIMATE	NEXT FISCAL YEAR — STAND DEV	NEXT FISCAL YEAR — NUMBER ESTIMATES	NEXT FISCAL YEAR — CHANGE MEAN (%)	NEXT 5 EPS GROWTH (%)
HUNTER ENVIRON	3/88	-0.16	MAR	N/A	0.45	N/A	1	0.0	N/A	N/A	0	0.0	N/A
HUNTINGDON INTL	9/88	1.69E	MAR	0.44	2.12	0.02	2	0.0	2.55	N/A	1	0.0	17.5
HUNTINGTON BANC	12/88	2.23	JUN	0.61	2.57	0.06	10	0.0	N/A	N/A	0	0.0	10.1
HUNTWAY PTNS LP	12/88	N/A E	MAR	N/A	0.83	N/A	1	0.0	N/A	N/A	0	0.0	N/A
HURCO COS INC	10/88	0.83	APR	0.32	1.60	0.10	2	3.9	2.00	N/A	1	0.0	20.7
HUTCHINSON TECH	9/88	1.09	MAR	0.26	-0.20	0.31	4	-260.0	1.00	N/A	1	0.0	N/A
HUTCHINSON WHAM	12/88	0.51E	MAR	N/A	0.63	N/A	1	0.0	N/A	N/A	0	0.0	N/A
HYDRAULIC CO	12/88	2.04	MAR	N/A	0.10	0.23	3	0.0	N/A	N/A	0	0.0	N/A
HYSAN DEVLPMT	12/88	0.09E	MAR	N/A	2.62	N/A	7	0.0	N/A	N/A	0	0.0	N/A
I E INDS	12/88	2.43	MAR	0.95	2.41	0.09	12	-0.5	2.35	N/A	1	0.0	3.5
IA-ILL GAS&EL	12/88	4.13E	MAR	N/A	4.18	0.08	7	0.0	4.30	N/A	1	0.0	3.6
IBERDUERO	12/88	0.50E	MAR	N/A	0.50	N/A	1	0.0	N/A	N/A	0	0.0	N/A
IBM	12/88	9.84	JUN	2.36	10.75	0.31	39	-1.1	11.66	0.48	21	-2.1	11.6
IBP INC	12/88	1.32	MAR	0.12	1.46	0.10	6	-2.7	1.70	0.06	4	1.5	12.0
ICH CORP	12/88	1.03E	MAR	0.15	1.38	0.81	5	-3.5	1.90	0.90	2	0.0	16.3
ICN PHARMACEUT	11/88	0.23	MAY	N/A	0.85	0.35	2	0.0	0.65	N/A	1	0.0	40.0
ICOT CORP	7/88	-0.57	APR	-0.10	-0.10	0.13	1	0.0	0.35	N/A	1	0.0	30.0
IDAHO POWER CO	12/88	1.32	MAR	0.42	1.96	0.08	16	-0.1	2.13	0.19	4	-22.3	4.2
IDB COMM	12/88	0.50E	MAR	0.10	0.62	N/A	4	-9.4	0.66	N/A	1	0.0	25.0
IDEAL BASIC IND	6/88	-0.11	MAR	N/A	1.19	N/A	1	0.0	N/A	N/A	0	0.0	16.0
IFR SYS INC	6/88	0.97	MAR	N/A	1.08	0.10	1	0.0	1.17	N/A	1	0.0	20.0
II-VI INCORP	6/88	0.51	JUN	N/A	0.60	0.16	1	0.0	N/A	N/A	0	-7.2	14.6
ILL TOOL WORKS	12/88	2.66	JUN	0.84	3.02	0.55	11	0.3	3.39	0.19	4	0.0	5.0
ILLINOIS CENTRL	12/88	1.38E	MAR	0.65	1.42	N/A	6	0.0	1.75	N/A	1	0.0	0.5
ILLINOIS POWER	12/88	1.66	MAR	0.25	2.07	0.05	20	-7.2	1.90	0.58	7	0.0	N/A
IMAGE RETAILING	6/88	N/A	MAR	0.01	0.08	N/A	1	0.0	0.05	N/A	1	0.0	N/A
IMAGINE FLM&ENT	9/88	N/A E	MAR	N/A	0.45	N/A	2	0.0	0.88	0.13	2	0.0	15.0
IMASCO LTD	12/88	2.51	MAR	1.60	2.80	0.23	11	-0.9	N/A	N/A	0	0.0	9.8
IMC FERTILIZER	6/88	N/A	JUN	N/A	5.92	0.03	9	0.0	7.21	0.33	10	-0.3	16.0
IMMUCOR	5/88	0.24	MAY	-0.11	-0.32	0.30	2	0.0	N/A	N/A	0	0.0	25.0
IMMUNEX CORP	12/88	0.07	MAR	N/A	-0.32	N/A	12	0.0	-0.24	0.22	5	0.0	N/A
IMMUNOMEDICS	6/88	-0.05E	MAR	0.52	-0.10	0.16	7	0.0	N/A	N/A	0	0.0	20.0
IMO IND	12/88	1.76	JUN	0.11	2.09	0.18	7	-0.9	2.41	0.04	2	-1.0	25.0
IMPACT SYS	3/88	0.27	MAR	N/A	0.17	N/A	1	0.0	2.75	N/A	1	0.0	N/A
IMPALA ADR	6/88	2.54E	MAR	2.52	2.45	0.26	13	4.0	N/A	N/A	0	0.0	N/A
IMPERIAL BCP	12/88	1.68	MAR	0.25	1.92	0.77	9	0.5	0.30	N/A	1	0.0	20.0
IMPERIAL CHEM	12/88	9.03E	MAR	0.93	9.85	1.04	13	-14.9	9.71	0.93	4	-1.0	11.2
IMPERIAL CORP A	12/88	0.71	JUN	N/A	2.28	0.63	1	-2.1	2.00	0.50	2	0.0	9.0
IMPERIAL OIL LT	12/88	2.35	MAR	N/A	3.34	N/A	14	-22.2	3.99	0.58	5	-10.3	9.0
IMRE CORP	12/88	-0.15E	MAR	N/A	0.35	N/A	2	0.0	2.00	N/A	0	0.0	N/A
IMREG INC A	7/88	-0.35E	MAR	0.22	-1.25	0.06	6	0.0	N/A	N/A	0	0.0	N/A
INACOMP COM CTR	12/88	0.66	APR	1.65	0.89	1.87	6	0.0	1.04	0.07	4	2.4	20.0
INCO LTD	12/88	6.50	JUN	0.12	6.05	0.01	14	1.0	4.05	2.08	6	0.0	6.7
INCSTAR CORP	3/88	0.26	MAR	N/A	0.56	N/A	2	0.0	0.84	0.08	2	0.0	24.0
INDEP BANKGROUP	12/88	2.01	MAR	1.00	2.25	0.11	6	0.0	N/A	N/A	0	0.0	N/A
INDEP INS GRP	12/88	3.94	MAR	N/A	4.38	0.40	6	0.0	4.65	N/A	1	0.0	7.6
INDEPENDENCE BK	12/88	-1.15	JUN	0.79	2.42	N/A	6	0.0	2.70	0.49	3	0.0	9.6

Figure Nine

had developed recently or, rather, had a long history. The number of calculations required for this process is staggering and well beyond the power of even the mightiest personal computer.

The final step in the process is the ranking of stocks. This tells the manager which to buy and which to sell. The stocks are classified by measuring expected return against required return (risk or volatility). Those stocks with "high expected return" and "low required return" receive a "Very High Rank," of which those in the top tenth percentile are bought. Conversely, stocks with a low expected return and a high required return reflect poor projections of future earnings or p/e ratios. These stocks receive a "Very Low Rank," and the bottom tenth percentile are sold short. The rest of the 3,000 stocks fall into the middle rankings, as shown in Figure Ten.

The Geewax, Terker system is a successful one, and it represents the changes in and the future of the investment business. It is a system that electronically and analytically searches for discrepancies in the pricing or valuations of stocks. The successful application of such techniques, at first reading, appears to fly in the face of our accepted theory that the markets are efficient. And, ironically, many of the quantitative models designed to search for market inefficiencies are developed by the same academics who first promulgated Modern Portfolio Theory and the notion that the markets are largely efficient.

	Low Expected Return	Average Expected Return	High Expected Return
Low Required Return	Average Rank	High Rank	Very High Rank
Average Required Return	Low Rank	Average Rank	High Rank
High Required Return	Very Low Rank	Low Rank	Average Rank

Figure Ten

We believe that both are facts: The markets *are* largely efficient, but discrepancies *do* exist between price and value, and these discrepancies can be located and taken advantage of. This can only work, however, in the aggregate groupings, for only in the aggregate can superior returns be achieved with acceptable risk levels. Modern money managers concur with this view. Even those who do not use sophisticated models like the Geewax, Terker example are using computers more and more often to sort through and find stocks that, when collected in one basket, will perform just as the market as a whole performs. These baskets are, naturally, the essence of program trading, and its speedy dominance of today's stock market would not have been possible without the computer.

Chapter Seven —————————————

PROGRAM TRADING AND THE CHANGING STOCK MARKETS

It was a wild year, 1987 was. But when all the furor settled and with the passage of time, it's pretty clear that the 1987 crash was *not* the harbinger of poor economic fundamentals that the crash of 1929 was to become.

A Convergence of Triggers

Can it happen again? Certainly. The future may be impenetrable, but it is possible that some unforeseeable combination of circumstances, as unimaginable as index options, program trading, and portfolio insurance were in 1929, could occur that would once again throw the financial markets into turmoil. Our view, however, is that such a combination would involve such extreme economic, political, and societal trauma (such as that occasioned by an outbreak of general war) that the health of the financial markets would be the public's least concern.

Will it happen again? No. The combination of circumstances that caused the severity of the market break of 1987 will not recur, whether or not government, regulators and the markets take any reforming steps in the wake of the market break.

The crash of 1987 was a unique phenomenon, because of the size of the market's downturn. But it does not represent any startling new truths about either investor perceptions or the state of the markets themselves. The SEC report on the Crash concluded that "the initial decline that immediately preceded the October 19 market break was triggered by investor perceptions regarding investment fundamentals and economic conditions."[1]

This implies that *suddenly*, for some strange reason, investors lost faith in the great bull market of the past five years. In fact, it was not a sudden occurrence: for months, money managers and analysts had been show-

---

[1] *The October 1987 Market Break*. A Report by the Division of Market Regulation, U.S. Securities and Exchange Commission, Feb. 1988 (Washington, DC: U.S. Government Printing Office), p. xiii.

ing their increasing concern that stock prices were too high and the market in general overinflated. Indeed, they had acted on this conviction by purchasing large amounts of portfolio insurance, which, as we have seen, is tantamount to making a bet that prices will fall. Had that bet and the size of the bet been made manifest at the time at which it was placed, the suddenness and, we believe, sharp magnitude of the crash would not have occurred. But instead, no one was watching or factoring in portfolio insurance until the time it actually "kicked in," October 19, and took its toll by sheer size and surprise.

The resulting decline of 22 percent largely resulted from the amounts of portfolio insurance activated on those days and the activities of traders reacting to that overhang. The question we have posed is: How, in the face of obvious investment fundamentals and economic conditions, were stock prices able to rise so high without the normal adjustments taking place? Normal adjustments mean selling. Under normal times investors would have begun selling as soon as they perceived prices were unseasonably high. But now, with portfolio insurance, they didn't have to make normal adjustments. They were guaranteed a sale at a particular moment at which a fail-safe point was reached. This was the ultimate trigger that caused the crash, and had there not been portfolio insurance the stock market wouldn't have risen so high. There were other conditions, though, as well, that if they did not actually trigger, still precipitated or caused the decline.

Merger and Acquisition Activity

A second element in the crash of '87 was the merger and acquisition activity in the economy, or, more accurately, the growing fear that that merger and acquisition activity soon would be curtailed. On the Wednesday before the crash, October 14, the House Ways and Means Committee reported out a tax bill that would have limited dramatically the deductibility of interest payments by corporations. If enacted, such a law would raise substantially the cost of capital for any corporation trying to finance a merger and acquisition.

The real boom period for merger and acquisition activity or "deals" or "deal stocks" as the game is named, was between 1985 and 1986. During that period both the number of deals valued over $1 million and the billions of dollars involved shot upwards. In 1980, only 50 deals with values of over $1 million were transacted. These had a total value of approximately $35 billion. By 1986, an estimated 4500 deals of over a million dollars were consummated, with a staggering $200 billion of total value.

In the real world, there is probably no better test for what a stock is worth than the price someone is willing to pay to buy the entire company. If the potential acquirer is hamstrung by a higher cost of capital, inevitably an adjustment will take place in the value of the stock of the company being considered for acquisition. This adjustment will be in a downward direction until the higher cost of capital has been compensated for by a lower purchase price. A mere *proposal* to raise the cost of capital would be enough to disrupt the markets. Those who would normally fund the debt part of the acquisition—commercial banks, investment banks, insurance companies, *et al*—would cease making commitments until final resolution of the question took place (*i.e.*, either a failure of the proposal to come out of committee, to pass a vote, or, on the other side, the enactment of it into law). And, in fact, soon after the action of the House Subcommittee became known, merger "foreplay" came to a halt. That was on October 14, 1987.[2]

The first parties to react to the cessation of deal-making activity were risk arbitrageurs. Although their names had been sullied by the rash of insider-trading cases, risk arbitrageurs have performed a real service to the marketplace for a long time by providing liquidity to the shareholders of companies being acquired or of companies viewed as likely prospects for acquisition. No matter what the eventual outcome, the arbitrageur plays an important role. If the deal is cancelled or if the so-called rumored deal stock never materializes as a genuine takeover candidate, the arbitrageur is the person to whom shareholders can go to sell the

---

[2] The SEC report *The October 1987 Market Break* (*op. cit.*, pp.3–10) noted that "preliminary data prepared by the Commission's Office of Chief Economist indicates a correlation between events concerning the tax bill and stock price movements during the market break" (including the fact that a subsequent "announcement by the Committee Chairman that he would agree to a reasonable compromise on the bill [was] followed by increases in stock prices").

stock, with the arbitrageur assuming the final risk should the deal not go through.

After October 14, risk arbitrageurs began to sell, as did other speculative holders of takeover stocks. Those stocks saw dramatic declines, and almost all the risk arbitrage firms realized heavy losses. We should note here also that when one company in a particular sector or industry becomes the target of a buyer, it sets a standard of valuation for the rest of the companies as well, even though they themselves are not candidates for acquisition. A subsequent cancellation of the take-over then reverberates throughout the entire industry, tending to devalue the stocks of all companies within that sector. This too happened in October 1987.

In 1988, the merger and acquisition activity picked up again, particularly after the House proposal was withdrawn. By the end of the year, total value of deals done was back up to over $200 billion, though the *number* of deals had dropped to pre-1984 levels. The deals were now fewer but bigger. In fact, 1988 became the year of the megadeal, led by RJR Nabisco at a whopping $25 billion. The sheer size of the RJR Nabis-co deal offer, plus the structure that would be used to implement the takeover—mostly debt with very little equity investment—has provoked a great deal of politi-cal and regulatory consideration of whether or not merger and acquisition activity is good for the economy and for our society as a whole. The subtext to that question is consideration of whether debt rather than equity as the prime source of financing does not indeed create a weakening within the financial structures of

American corporations. And an added undertone to the debt question is provided by the fact that much of the debt-financing has been in the form of high-yield bonds, known as junk bonds, which then must be digested by the markets.

What do junk bonds and interest deductibility have to do with program trading and the changing stock market? Public policy decisions that affect something as fundamental as the cost of capital will have a dramatic effect on the volatility of the stock market. Investors, sensing the likelihood of more expensive capital either will hedge their currently held stock positions against that event by selling the futures or will sell the future, even without owning the stock, simply as a way of profiting from the eventual decline. Either way, the effect is the same: The price of the future falls, dropping to a discount of its fair value. At this point enters the index arbitrageur, who buys the future and sells off the stocks through the instrument of a program trade, thus driving down stock prices; this is exactly what happened in October 1987.

Market Regulation

October 1987 showed that the nation's financial system of markets was vulnerable to a breakdown. On those days, as we have seen, the varying markets—stock, stock index futures, and stock options—all interacted freely with each other, but the result was a disaster. In the wake of that disaster arises the question of the role played by law and regulation and whether changes should be made in the present balance that exists between government intervention and the free markets. Program trading and the increasing institutionalization of investment decisions and strategies prompts, in some quarters, consideration of whether the financial markets have outgrown the regulatory structures designed to aid their free movement. The historical context offers some perspectives on the issue.

Where demand and supply exist in sufficient quantity, a marketplace will soon arise to ease the flow of supply to demand, to provide liquidity. So it was in the grain markets of the ancient world, where demand was so great that it justified the building of 400-foot freighters for the seasonal trade across the Mediterranean. And so it was in Holland's "tulipomania," where exchanges sprang up solely to deal in tulip bulbs or, more interestingly, options and futures for tulip bulbs. Defaults on the latter, as the bubble peaked, hastened its collapse.

This was true as well in the fledging United States, as nineteenth century economic expansion created demand for credit, investment and, in due course, transfer of risk from producers and users to financial intermediaries. Banking, the stock markets, and the commodities markets thus arose, grew and prospered, pretty much in isolation from one another as each served its own specialized area. The banks provided credit; the stock markets channeled investment; the commodities markets transferred risk. They still do;

the broad lines of financial activity have not changed, as the different regulatory agencies that have evolved to oversee each financial sector make clear. The stock, futures, and options exchanges establish and enforce the rules for the stock and derivative products markets respectively. Over those exchanges sit federal regulatory commissions which require or approve changes in rules as well as monitor the exchanges self-regulation. The Securities and Exchange Commission oversees the stocks and options markets while the Commodity Futures Trading Commission is responsible for the futures market.

The lines have blurred from time to time, however. Following every financial crisis, panic or crash, blame was placed on some overstepping of the boundaries between the various financial sectors. Each such event spawns rules, regulations, legislation and procedures that with the great clarity of hindsight attempt to prevent a similar situation from arising in the future.

The National Banks of the United States were legislated into existence during the Civil War to meet the needs of an expanding and industrializing nation for which the older banking system no longer served adequately. The Federal Reserve System came into being in 1913 to correct problems that had grown up in the National Banking system. In this manner, the United States finally acquired a central bank. The banking acts of the 1930s addressed situations that the original Federal Reserve Act had never foreseen. New legislation enforced a split between the banking industry and the securities industry, through the Banking Act of

1933 (Glass-Steagall Act), established a host of bank regulatory bodies and set up the Securities and Exchange Commission.

The regulatory agencies and federal and state laws evolved over time to meet perceived needs in the area of fiscal policy and, particularly, to prevent abuses in the financial markets. Regulation and legislation usually developed out of crisis, either long-term, much as the one that gave rise to the Federal Reserve systems, or sudden and violent, such as the crash of 1929 (factually the culmination of a long-standing policy of laissez-faire) and the subsequent Great Depression.

The legacy of the New Deal, with its array of regulatory and statutory programs and policies, remains the most significant as far as the financial markets and institutions are concerned. In a very real sense, the separateness of the various financial bodies and markets, which over time had been moving into one another's areas, was confirmed and solidified. Distinct regulatory organizations for the commodities and futures markets, the equity markets, and the banks ensured that these different entities would function pretty much exclusively in their own domains.

Of course, the financial community is interlinked at many levels. Banks provide credit to brokers and commodity traders. Commodity and futures markets assume risk for corporations whose stock and debt instruments are floated on, and trade in, the equities markets.

Before Glass-Steagall, there was no distinction between an investment bank and a commercial bank. Banks took depositors' funds, made loans, bought and sold securities, underwrote the equity issues of corporations and funded the investment community. These functions grew naturally out of the banking system's historical role in providing liquidity to the community, the inheritance of the merchant banking houses of Europe. Those banks, going back to antiquity, provided all financial services and they still do. The legal distinction between commercial banking and investment banking does not exist in most other countries, though in fact many banks choose to be one or the other rather than both. In the U.S., Glass-Steagall separated the two decisively. Securities firms or investment banks were forbidden from accepting commercial deposits and withdrawals; commercial banks could not buy, sell or underwrite corporate stocks for their own accounts.

That same year, Congress enacted the Securities Act of 1933 to deal with fraudulent and unethical practices witnessed in the years leading up to the great crash. The 1933 Act was superseded one year later by the more encompassing Securities Exchange Act of 1934. This law created the SEC and provided the framework for defining and correcting unethical trading practices and manipulation of the stock markets. These three New Deal pieces of legislation remain in place today and constitute the fundamental governing principles that regulate the securities industry.

The world moves ahead in a smooth continuum or a series of many small incremental changes. Systems established to deal with the world as it is today may begin to become obsolete tomorrow. Over time, the best systems, built on the best hindsight, are often seriously out of date, geared to problems that no longer exist or unable to cope with ones undreamed of when the system was installed.

The systems put in place during the 1930s have served the public and the financial markets well. The nation has weathered many economic crises without serious damage. But the programs of the New Deal were essentially Keynesian, created to deal with an economy in Depression and plagued by deflation and unemployment, with stagnant or falling production. Despite frequent adjustments through legislation and regulatory rulings, the Depression-born governmental structures designed to monitor the financial industry have not kept in step with the real world.

At the onset of the 1982 bull market, the financial markets were still undergoing perhaps the most fundamental alterations since their inception. These changes included the shift from individual to institutional investors as the primary participants, computerization, and the enormous increase both in daily trading volume and in the size of blocks routinely traded. Foremost was the development of new instruments and investment strategies, the rise of index funds, and the beginning of program trading in its several forms. The existing market and its 50-year old regulatory structure had neither anticipated nor prepared for this tidal wave of change.

Regulating or Reforming Volatility

Volatility has emerged as perhaps the major concern of both market professionals and the public. The concern is not new. Shakespeare put it well in *The Merchant of Venice*, set in the fourteenth century: "but even now worth this, and now worth nothing?" Salerio was a speculator having all his eggs in one basket or, rather, all his goods in one bottom. His friend Antonio, however, was an early asset allocator:

> My ventures are not in one bottom trusted,
> Nor to one place; nor is my whole estate
> Upon the fortune of this present year;

In the end, Salerio's single ship came safely home, while against the odds all Antonio's ventures failed. Both Antonio and Salerio knew the odds. At the beginning of play, Salerio is apprehensive about his ship whereas Antonio is quite sanguine about his allocated assets. But odds being odds, sometimes the 100-to-1 shot comes in while the 1-to-5 loses, both in the fourteenth century and today. Today's speculator, hoping to win big on a single large investment, however, can still expect a whipping from volatility, while the asset allocator can smooth the fluctuations in one investment with contrary ones in another.

Volatility's theoretical relationship to risk, its real link to investor perceptions of risk, its degree as a function of information transfer, and its place in Mod-

191

ern Portfolio Theory are all very well. But the average investor, on looking at his portfolio between October 16 and October 20, was much more likely to say, "Then worth that, and now worth only this?"

Volatility matters most to people and institutions who trade often. While it is a measure of risk, in that its magnitude reflects investor skittishness concerning the effect of news on the future price of the security, it is also a measure of information transfer.

In a truly efficient market where all information about a security that can affect its price is instantly available, the price will constantly change to reflect newly arriving information. The price may move rapidly, but it will move in small increments and quickly reach a new level. Separate from the information-caused price move is investor perception of the stock—the degree to which a specific piece of information moves a specific stock. That degree of move is the stock's natural volatility, the beta of Modern Portfolio Theory.

We see an enormous confusion in the marketplace and even among the regulators and the many commissions and reports on the issue of volatility. The SEC report, for example, says, "We recognize that in one sense volatility is a neutral phenomenon: a measure of how quickly prices react to new information." It would be more accurate to say that volatility is a measure of how quickly prices react to the *lack* of information.

In an efficient market, new information translates instantly into price changes. Normally, these price changes are small. In a perfectly efficient market with complete and instantaneous information transfer, price changes would follow a smooth continuum as information that affects investor perception of future prospects is constantly received and processed.

Occasionally, some momentous piece of information will so change perceptions that the stock or the market will make a major move. Observers say "volatility" and blame better and faster communications and information transfer. They may be correct in stating that fast assimilation of information caused the price change but wrong in calling it volatility. A single move in either direction is not volatility. Volatility is a number of such moves over time, enough of them to establish a pattern and generate data from which people can calculate ratios, numbers, norms, means, averages, and the like. Blaming sudden large changes on the outbreak of news overlooks the far more liquid, non-volatile, more smoothly functioning, correctly priced day-to-day market that better information assures.

Volatility is by definition a relative thing. Markets fluctuate. However, few would deny that 500 points or 22 percent is too large a fluctuation. The SEC report says why:

> When price swings reach extreme levels, they can have a number of adverse consequences. First, such volatility increases marketmaking risks and

requires market intermediaries to charge more for their liquidity services, thereby reducing the liquidity of the market as a whole. Second, if such volatility persists, securities firms are less able to use their available capital efficiently because of the need to reserve a larger percentage of cash-equivalent investments in order to reassure lenders and regulators. Third, greater volatility can reduce investor confidence in investing in stocks. As a result of these effects, we believe substantially increased price volatility could, in the long run, impact the ability of U.S. corporations to raise capital efficiently through the sale of equity securities. [3]

Information Can Regulate Volatility

But what is excess volatility? And for whom is it excess? Is it 100 points, or 50, or 10? In 1988, the NYSE decided that more than 50 points was too much. Given the level of the Dow at that time, the Exchange deemed a movement of about 2.5 percent to be excessive. At that level, the NYSE forbade use of the SuperDOT system for program trading when a day's fluctuation exceeded 50 points. But why not 40 points, or 60, or a percentage of the day's opening index?

---

[3] "Report of the Presidential Task Force on Market Mechanisms," January 1988, Executive Summary, p. xii.

Given the enormous trading volume in today's markets and the presumably greater volume to come in tomorrow's, it is essential that all market participants be able to have access to all pertinent information as rapidly as possible. Information in this sense does not refer merely to economic news and specific details about stocks and factors that may affect stock prices. In the age of the composite asset and program trading, information includes data concerning the markets themselves.

For example, a traditional and useful way for investors to protect themselves against excessive loss in the equities markets is to place a stop-loss order with the broker. The stop-loss will instruct the specialist to sell the stock at the customer's price, or as close to it as possible. The customer may set this price at any level, or may set it as trailing stop-loss which will always be behind the stock price by, say, 10 percent. Should the stock lose 10 percent of its value, the customer's profit is protected to that extent and the shares will be sold at that price.

Stop-loss orders do pose some problems for the investor. In a rapidly moving market, the price may drop below the order before it can be executed. In a volatile stock, the customer may be whipsawed out of the stock as the price dips briefly below the stop-loss level, then rebounds. However, stop-loss orders are entered in the specialists' books and are a matter of record. The specialist can estimate the downward pressure that cascading stop-loss orders could exert.

The stop-loss order is to the individual investor what portfolio insurance is to the institutional investor. The stop-loss order has no premium cost, only the risk that the investor will be inadvertently sold out. (And, as we have described, even the individual investor has more sophisticated tools at his disposal for counterbalancing this risk. He can hedge with index options to protect a good part of the portfolio's value. That strategy, of course, has a cost—the option expenses—but it allows the investor to keep the portfolio regardless of fluctuations in value.)

Where the potential effects of stop-loss and other limit orders can be gauged because the orders are entered on specialists' books and thus knowable, the potential of portfolio insurance and other hedging strategies that depend on links between the equities and futures markets cannot be known.

Two factors keep the potential liability of portfolio insurance hidden. One is that, unlike stop and limit orders, no record exists in the market. The strategies reside off the trading floor or out of the trading system until they are triggered. "Portfolio insurance . . . is handled by an upstairs firm and does not provide any prior warning of the amount of potential selling it represents—either to the specialist or other market participants," says the SEC report.

The existence of formal portfolio insurance managers who administer the strategies as an overlay on the insured fund has provided some idea of the amount of dynamic insurance hedging that could come into action

196

in a down market. But the fact that the Brady Commission report was unable to state by even a large margin how much insurance overhung the market before October indicates the uncertainty and the scope of the problem.

Open information, openly disclosed, strikes us as the best regulator of fair and orderly markets. It is the ultimate antidote to volatility and it has worked whenever it's been honestly tried. The volatility that used to be seen on Triple Witching Days, when the whole market could move up or down by as much as 40 points in the final few minutes before expiration, was sharply reduced by requiring that buyers and sellers disclose their plans one-half hour before the close. Now, in that final half-hour, the only players allowed in are those taking the opposite or "balancing" side of the last stated position.

We believe that this same type of disclosure requirement should be applied to other now-hidden strategies, portfolio insurance chief among them. We think that the market, if not the regulators, will soon demand for its own efficiency accurate and timely information about who has portfolio insurance programs in place and what the aggregate size is of that "potential" sale. That information will become as important a part of the market's data base as disclosure of short interest in trades made by corporate officials is now. We urge that up-to-date portfolio insurance reporting be made a regulatory priority. It will help guarantee that another severe market break will never happen.

Similar disclosure should be made of other institutional strategies as they are adopted or put into place.

Let's take the example of leveraged buy-outs. At year end 1988 a survey conducted by *Pensions & Investment Age* revealed that among the top 200 pension funds in the country, $3.5 billion was invested in leveraged buyouts.[4] What is not known is how much money has been committed to additional investment in LBOs. Typically, managers of LBO funds use the instrument of limited partnerships to organize their investment activities. As part of making an investment in the limited partnership, investors would make a commitment for a specified amount of money that would be drawn down as the LBO fund manager completed a transaction. Thus, while we know that these top 200 funds have $3.5 billion already invested, we do not know how much has been contractually committed for future investment. In the structure of a leverage buyout transaction, investment dollars can be leveraged as much as two times. So if these 200 funds should be committed to another $3.5 billion of investment, the LBO fund managers would possess $35 billion of buying power in the marketplace. The presence of this buying power is inherently an enormous bullish factor for the stock market. Conversely, if for some political reason, the enormous buying power constituted by LBO commitments were to be eliminated, that would have a considerably negative effect on the entire market.

---

[4] *Pensions & Investment Age*, Jan. 23, 1989.

As a matter of public policy, limited partnerships that are formed by sufficiently few individuals are not subjected to regulatory scrutiny, although in some states a sense of the scope of funds committed for varying purposes can be fathomed (albeit with difficulty) from information required by the particular state. In the case of LBO limited partnerships, we can see how a small number of institutional investors, by virtue of the magnitude of their commitment, can create a vehicle capable of having dramatic impact on the stock market.

It is not our aim to advocate regulating the investment activities of LBO pools. We do believe, however, that information about the magnitude of their possible activities should be made available (that is, disclosed) to everyone. In sum: The easy flow of information is essential to the smooth operation of the markets. In any situation where commitments, if implemented, would have a significant effect on the market, those commitments, like portfolio insurance, should be made known. This philosophy should be applied across the board, from the macrocosm of portfolio insurance to the microcosm of the specialist's trading book in a single stock.

Program Trading Is Here to Stay

Readers should not expect program trading in any of its forms to be outlawed. Nor will the derivative instruments be proscribed. On the contrary, we expect to see more of them based on other indexes, as well as more of them in overseas financial markets. These instruments have become part of the financial toolbox. They may be misused or not used but they can no longer be discarded.

Their proper use, however, requires a one-market view with faultless communications and linkages between the equities markets and the derivative markets. That linkage was missing for at least some of the time on October 19 and 20, and it was that lack of linkage—lack of information through which market participants could properly price and act—that contributed to the speed and magnitude of the market break. When the linkage between the stock market, the futures market and the options market is unobstructed, the liquidity in one market enhances the liquidity in another. And liquidity of the entire system is the result.

Those market participants who constitute the linkage between the markets are not without responsibility. And they are subject to guidelines. These participants are, by name, the arbitrageurs who buy in one market, like the futures or options market, and then sell in the equities market through use of a program trade. By definition, an arbitrageur must buy and sell the same entity (though it can be in different form) simultaneously. If the sale and purchase are not executed simultaneously and one position is taken at a time after the other, risk is involved. What has happened in the markets is that classic arbitrage (arbitrage, by definition is riskless) has been corrupted, turned into a "pseudo-arbitrage" type of program trading (a popular form of it called "legging") whereby traders take one side of the position minutes or even hours before executing the other side. The overload contributes to market volatility by placing extra pressure on the futures and stock prices of companies whose securities often do not see very much action. On January 8, 1988, such legging sent the Dow down 140 points, with overwhelming selling (but no buying, which true arbitrageurs would have done) on the part of traders, many of them acting for their own accounts and ahead of their clients' interest.

Many recommendations for change seek to tinker with the instruments when, as in this illustration, there are some players whose activities should be tinkered with. We think nothing is wrong with the instruments. Nor do we believe the basic system to be seriously deficient.

Most of the suggestions made by the various panels and commissions would restrict free operation of the markets in some manner. Suggestions include trading halts, price movement limits, restrictions on program trading when the market moves more than a certain amount in a day, margin requirements for futures equivalent to those required for stocks, settlement of index futures and options in kind rather than in cash, movement of futures trading to the stock exchanges, a super-agency to oversee all financial markets, better coordination between the futures and equities markets, better oversight and control of specialists and market makers, higher capital requirements, quicker access to capital, a basket trading desk on the New York Stock Exchange, and more. Some of these have merit and some will come to pass, without government fiat. Despite considerable clamor to hurry up and do something about what occurred on October 19, there appears to be tremendous inertia about doing anything just yet. The essence of the financial markets is free and open competition to arrive at fair pricing. There is enormous reluctance to make any moves that would disturb that essence and perhaps badly fix something that isn't broken.

Program Trading and the Individual Investor

Program trading did not cause the October 1987 market break. The strategy was a handy culprit in the midst of the carnage, especially when well-placed people in the financial markets pointed in that direction. Every study since done on the crash, as well as earlier ones dealing with high-volatility trading, absolved program trading of responsibility for causing the collapse. Portfolio insurance, however, turned out to be a greater culprit than at first thought. But it acted on a process that was already well underway.

What does this mean to the average non-professional investor? Practically speaking, nothing.

Program trading in the form of portfolio repositioning or index arbitrage has no relevance at all to the mass of investors. This is trading that puts into practice the idea of the composite asset, a basket of stocks whose value far exceeds the means of most individual investors. Individuals with interests in pension plans, mutual funds, and the like, of course, do benefit, through their fund holdings, from any efficiencies, savings, and additional earnings fund managers can generate with such strategies.

Nonprofessional investors should consider program trading in all its forms as just another technique the professionals use to maximize gains and minimize losses. Individuals benefit, through better pricing for their own securities and greater liquidity.

But program trading is quite simply not a strategy in which the ordinary investor can participate. Program trading is now a fact of the market life that has been integrated into the mainstream of stock market practice. Some rules and regulations may eventually be imposed, but we believe such rules will most carefully avoid interfering with the free movements of the market.

The best way to deal with program trading is to accept it as a fact of financial life. One invests to earn a risk-adjusted return over time. It is impossible to know whether the market will be up or down next week, next month or next year, and how much. But it is a certainty that over time the market indexes will increase in line with the expansion in the gross national product, corporate profits, and inflation. Some years the index curve will be above that combined figure and some years below. But the trend will be consistently up as long as the economy itself grows.

Our final advice to the private investor is to accept the reality of the indexes and buy the entire market. We have explored in this book all the whys and hows, and it's all quite attainable. And then one day, when your neighbor says about a company that's just been part of a megadeal, "Boy, I wish I had owned that stock before the deal," you'll be able to say honestly, "I *did* own some of it."

INDEX